FOUR YEARS IN JAIL

A COLLECTION OF SHORT STORIES BY ROHIT DASH

SUKOMAL DASH

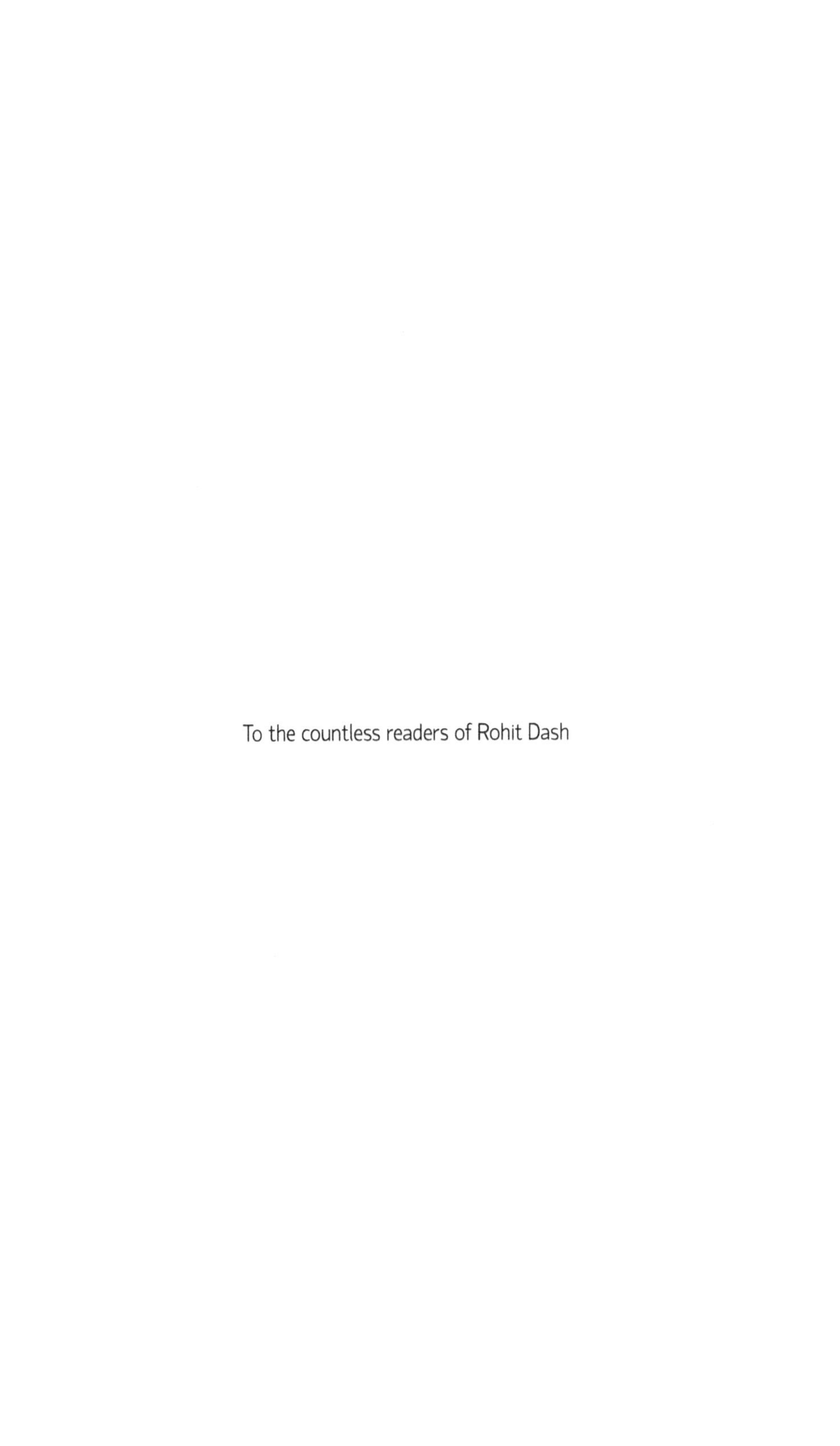

To the countless readers of Rohit Dash

Contents

Acknowledgements

Thank you Prasim Swaroop
for a nice cover design
and the publication support

CHAPTER ONE

Cockroach

Emerges a pair of antennae, gently from the hole, close to the doorjamb. Squiggles a bit. Surfaces a head, looks around and retreats into the hole.

Satyajit opens the window. Looks out, towards the sky a bit, closes the window and rolls over the bed. He brings about a book from beneath the pillow, leafs through two to three pages, exhales a long sigh of despair, arranges the pillow a bit against the wall, places the book over the bed and stares straight.

The wall is before his eyes. Cobwebs fill the wall. Layers of dust over the books have depleted their titles. So much of gossamer cover the frame holding that, his own face has almost merged with the insect, tangling in its own delicate fabric.

The cockroach gently crawls out of the hole. Looks around. Cautiously climbs the wall, but skids. Again climbs, again skids, yet carries on the exercise. Come may any tempest or tornado, it will not be crushed. How at last, climbs the cockroach up the wall, Satyajit recalls the story as told by his granny and repeated falls of late is a wont with him.

The cockroach roams around the house. It enters the books and comes out of the trousers and shirts, dangling from the rack. Entering the leaves of the calendar, it creates a rustling noise. Hides it at some obscure place for a bit and reappears from below the bed. Climbs it over Satyajit, crawls for a span and regresses to its darkness.

Satyajit puts his dress on. Getting out of his gloomy by-lane he covers a span of the street. Where will he go? Why did he get out at all? Where was he supposed to head? Fails he to find a purpose. He walks down a bit more. Returning, he sits at the tea shop.

People walk down the street dragging their *chappals*.What is there behind their heavy layer of make up? Is the decked up girl pretty? Would she be having a suitor or would any one be loathing on her?

Again Satyajit would think, why at all did he come here? Is it essential to sit here? Did he finish his tea up? Now, what does he do? He gets up. Clueless he is. He heads for the railway station.

Stands he before the booking window. 'I don't have to go anywhere.' People book tickets as per their need. The bugle of the train is audible. Rises up the hubbub. Satyajit rushes inward. The sky is overcast with smoke of diesel. Words of mouth trim down. Stands the train still like a tamed horse. Blinks it on to the dense darkness ahead. Rests for a while. Peeping at the pretty faces peeking through the window and brooding over the passengers dangling from the compartment doors, Satyajit waddles ahead. Stretch out hands through windows for bidding farewell. Amidst some cheerful faces and greater number of grieving faces overcast with sorrows, hands wave. Satyajit also waves his hand. Arrival of none expected, departure of none as well, none there to return him a wave of hands – on to road, Satyajit is back. Struggling through the crowd he returns, counting the number of jeeps, cars, trucks and buses parked beside the street.

What does the cockroach do once it is back in its dingy hole? How deep does the hole stretch, where does it end, does it open up to another outlet? Do cockroaches breathe? Are they vertebrate or invertebrate? Does a cockroach have kith or kin or all alone it is? What do they nibble in the hole, do they ever fall ill? How long do they live and what do they do? Why do they survive, do they only take birth and die? Is their birth essential? In spite of having so many legs, why do they need wings? It is these wings that Satyajit is so furious of cockroaches.

While flipping through the Zoology book, he ponders: why was he born? What was the need? Why is he alive? What is the need? How long is he going to live, what will he do, what will cease but for his survival, what was lacking, when he was not born?

Satyajit opens up the box. Noting down his date of birth from the Matric Certificate, he counts his age. Thirty years. How did a few years vanish in between? He had counted his age to be twenty-seven then. Just one last year left to sit for competitive tests. He had appeared the tests. Neither the results came out nor there any communication. Not a thing he remembers now, regarding those tests. Why does it happen of late? Everything goes wrong. He recalls not a thing, did something happen to him?

Satyajit stands before the mirror. Is his face suitable for his thirty years of age? Two blinking eyes buried in cavity beside a long nose. Cutting the straight line of the two eyes at right angle, from the base of the nose, two arcs of eye brows. Beyond the rectangular forehead, on the head, an insect infested crop of hair. Asked Satyajit to self, "Is it I? How was my previous look, should I refer to my old photo album? What's the need?" He retreats on to his bed.

Perhaps the cockroach had no kin. Occasionally it used to vanish. Unless Satyajit sees it for a while, he starts thinking, probably it fell ill or died in its hole or may be lying dead outside. Or, did it go away somewhere? Why at all should he chew over it for so long? Satyajit diverts his mind onto something else.

Who are the kith or kin Satyajit has? He recalls the facial features of his parents. How long has he been away from home? He decides to go home this Sunday.

Do cockroaches have parents? Poor fellow, it mustn't have any relation. At times Satyajit feels sorry for it and faces a dilemma, whenever he mulls to call it by a name, out of affection. Is the cockroach a female or male? Male or female, how is it determined in their case? All their faces are similar. What is there in a name? It's all the same, to have a name or not.

Repeatedly Satyajit considers a trip for home but succeeds not. Sometime he fails to get up on time, at times he feels lazy, even at times he returns from the bus stand out of boredom and reflects, all the same it is. Living anywhere is all the same. Would his mother be missing him? Would his father be remembering him? Why need they grieve for him? Why should he live for others? Would he have wished for his birth if permitted? He is suffocating, ruminating such countless whys, why shouldn't he focus on something else? Only by brooding over endless whys, impossible it's to reach a conclusion. Will he go mad? This time, before going home, he must pay a visit to some hospital. Why do I fail to love any body?

The cockroach was now hanging out with another cockroach. For long periods they were staying together. Perhaps the other one was a new comer from some near by neighbourhood. After some long socialisation they were now in the room of Satyajit. The first one doesn't roam these days as it did earlier. Usually they keep facing each other probably kissing.

Satyajit thinks, probably the cockroach got married.

Do cockroaches love? Do they tie the knot? What's their marriageable age? Do cockroaches have hearts? What's the difference between the heart of the Zoology book and a loving heart? Intending to write down a few lines, Satyajit takes out his pen and paper. It's all the same, there is no love. Loads of rubbish has been written as romantic poems. There is nothing more to write, not a word, better to read, better to read, it's all the same, better to sip a cup of tea.

Satyajit dresses up and goes to the tea stall. Drinking there three cups of tea he returns back. He washes down his hands and feet and kneeling down in the central room, sits with palms folded on his chest.

What would God be doing now? Whatever he says, will it be audible to Him now? Who is God? Why should he implore Him?

Again Satyajit ponders, lest He should be there? Lest he should be listening to everything? If He were there, what is the harm in praying him, if He were not there, let He not be there.

Dear bro! I am a miserable man. May you hear me a bit. It's most unfortunate that I myself don't know where my problem lies. Who am I? Why did I come, what am I doing, and what need I do? After imploring so much, thought Satyajit, should he offer a bung and again thought over the love, fear, heart, sorrows of the cockroaches, it's all the same.

Satyajit thought, either he should get married or at least he should have a courtship. Does his age justify for courtship any more? At what age such relations happen? Do old people go for courtship? Is he old enough? When does man grow old? Why does one grow old? Suppose after courtship I don't marry? If I continue courting even after marriage, whom shall I court with? If I marry straight away? If not, why not, if I carry on only courting, but why?

Considering writing down an essay on it, counting whether to write in favour or against it, he writes down: man is a brute. He fails to add anything new. All the knowledge are second-hand acquired, rote-learnt from books: marriage is a social malady. Will it be popular? Again he ponders and fixes his gaze on the wall, it's all the same, all the cockroaches are same, no... neither breath in nostrils, nor throb of pulse or heat of life, cockroaches are all the same. He gazes at the wall and again utters.

I don't have to speak any thing on any topic to anybody. Whatever I am speaking is truth. Henceforth from tomorrow, I will stop thinking on anything, on anybody. I am doing as per my sweet will, I have no message.

Still the next day Satyajit pondered. How long do cockroaches survive? Putting his dress on, he went out, what do cockroaches do? He rolled upon his bed on return, do cockroaches have dreams? Power was out. Groping in the darkness as he fumbled, under his slipper something cracked and Satyajit shuddered. May it be a human being, may it be a peanut peel, but may live on the cockroach, he wished.

Satyajit attempts to write a condolence message, prior to the autopsy of the cockroach. The other cockroach hovers over the carcass like a nutter even dashed at Satyajit's body. Howling out of fear, Satyajit rushes out, shaking his dress.

The cockroach is still hovering over his body. In the night, everywhere around his mosquito net, there has been a severe infestation of cockroaches, trying to push into the mosquito net. He was drenched in sudor. Intending to quit this house as he starts rolling his bedding, collecting his books and other materials, he looked out of the window and turned his eyes on to the wall. Ants were dragging the carcass of the cockroach on the floor. Satyajit went out and returned after hanging around a bit. He unrolled his bedding, spread and rolled on it.

The other cockroach showed forth its pair of antennae from the hole close by the doorjamb. Squiggled a bit. Surfaces the head out, looks around and into the hole retreats.

Satyajit opens up the window. Looks out, at the sky a bit. Closes the window and putting on his dress, crossing the gloomy by-lane, stands on the street. All the same it is. All the cockroaches are same. What is my need to come here, he ponders? Now, where do I go? It is all the same. I shall move on.

CHAPTER TWO

Snake

Mohanty babu was not like this before as he is now. He was a man of serious demeanour. Seldom did he smile without sufficient reason. His smiles were well measured. He didn't rear any bad habits. He maintained a good distance from *pān*, *biḍi*, cigarettes and tobacco. A teetotaller, rarely he chewed a cardamom seed, even when offered. He kept confined to self and stayed away from others' affairs or denigrates anybody. Needlessly he neither spoke to his neighbours nor even looked at their face. By chance, if in some market place a neighbour bumped into him and asked about his well being, failing to identify the person, he retreated with a forced half smile. He would not offer self, even a chance to think about the person, as to who he was or when or where did they meet.

Mohanty Babu was always busy, either in his official or domestic or personal chores. He attended neither any funeral nor any auspicious ceremony. He didn't have time to attend to any guest or mind trouble of anybody. Yes, it is the same Mohanty Babu, who is casual with others, a bit absent minded, a bit emotional, carrying always an undesired graveness on his face. In spite of the man being candid, neighbours level him to be an arrogant soul, though envy his personality.

Nothing would have changed and his life would have taken its usual smooth course, had a snake not crept into his life. This snake upset his whole life.

Everything deranged the moment, when writing a report to update his C.C.R. in the office, he learnt that his age has crossed forty. In an instant, he saw twinkling insects circling his vision and the letters of the news papers blurred before his eyes. All the close by articles seemed to him obscure and tasteless. Even, he could not see his loving family members like his parents, brothers, sisters, wife or children from close quarter. Thus, to have a view of them, he needed to stand at a precise distance.

This account of age, put him in a state of dilemma. His occasional smiles lost. 'How long more shall I survive? What is the average human life span; sixty, fifty or less? How long my service period is left? Do I have enough savings? What will happen to my beautiful wife? Clad in a white saree can she manage or will she indulge in immoral relations after sending the children to school? What rubbish! Can't she do all these now even? Is she doing all that? It's all baseless suspicion, sinful thoughts, saves me O God! Save me from all these iniquitous thoughts.'

At the same time he felt his wife as if unattached to him. 'No more overflows her earlier love. Somehow, she has slackened a lot. Is it all symptoms of my advancing age?' Again Mohanty Babu rubbished all such unwanted thoughts. 'Aged enough you are my dear, enough is enough. Meditate on *RāmaNāma* henceforth,' he counselled himself feeling dejected. Still reciting from '*Manabodha Chautiṣā*' in mind, Mohanty Babu slipped into a slumber, with a feeling of deep mental agony.

While watering the plants in the garden, he came across a copper coloured serpent hissing at him, spreading its hood. He was shocked. Mustering courage, soon he started backing out. Dot on time, the small water pot slipped off his hand. Anticipating the enemy close by, the serpent suddenly jumped at him. Mohanty Babu had no chance even to hold his *lungi* in place and he ran half naked shouting snake, snake, snake at the top of his voice, his heart beat touching an incredible pace.

The morning broke with such a nightmare. The neighbourhood rooster had repeated its cock-a-doodle-doo cries. The pet parrot's *'trāhi kara, trāhi kara'* (save us, save us) call was resounding in the atmosphere. Still his wife and children were fast asleep peacefully. Mohanty Babu sat up on the bed startled, shook himself, and surveyed all around the bed. No, there was no serpent or snake or any thing like that. Content, he tried to sleep again. But shit! the same nightmare didn't leave him.

This time, the snake was not in the garden, but it was slithering out of his bed room like a stealer. The attire of his wife messed up and she was fast asleep as if satisfied and fatigued due to an overwhelming coition.

Mohanty Babu again looked at the face of the snake intensely. Oh shit! It's a known face. Who is that; his neighbour, or his colleague, or the tutor of his son, or his bosom friend Umesh, or his cousin, or the domestic help? No, he is unable to make out the face, yet the arena of suspicion was expanding. Even though he cannot discern accurately, the bastard does resemble some one, well acquainted with him and boldly opening the door to get out, as if it were his paternal house.

Mohanty Babu's anger rose beyond limit. He searched out for a stick. No, it seems there is no stick or one of the sort in this house. Only there are four numbers of them, all fixed to the bed, to hold the mosquito net. The last, the only thick one, is fixed behind the back door, to safeguard the house from burglars. Is there any thing of the sort in this house? Losing his patience as Mohanty Babu ran to snatch a stick fixed to the bed, the snake got off and his slumber broke at the reproach of his wife. Oh, shit! What a nightmare. Mohanty Babu gazing at the face of his wife sceptically went to the bathroom to relieve himself.

That snake, that hypothetical snake, spoiled everything. Since that day, Mohanty Babu remained upset. He found the snake on the face of everyone who came in his contact. While walking down the road, he startled hallucinating a rope as a snake. He felt a snake erecting it's hooded head from his office file. A snake appeared to him at the window of his house. While in office, whenever he thought of his home, he felt as if a snake is resting on his bed comfortably. He jumped at home and in office fantasising snake. The snake, the snake of this day dream bewildered him.

One afternoon he came home under the pretext of lunch. The entrance door was half open. Mohanty Babu cautiously tiptoed in. Carefully he advanced near the window of the bedroom. Very slowly he opened up the doors of the window and screamed snake... snake... The neighbours who came running hearing Mohanty Babu's scream, found him tightly holding his wife's throat. With much effort they separated him and handed over to the police.

While Mohanty Babu considered himself hale and hearty, others had termed him to be mentally sick and rest part of his life he spent that way.

CHAPTER THREE

The weaver bird's nest

Why after all, did they choose a rented house in such a place? Not a single proper soul was available for a chit chat to pass time. Stepping out of home, one tumbles into stakes of rubbish, wastes, stinky gutter, tottering huts, useless lowly folks. Open up the windows and listen only to vulgar brawls, abusive scuffles of the neighbours. Not a bit of open space, for the child to play. Once the kid goes out, one needs to keep an eye on him. Such a tiny township that, it lacks space even for a stroll. Sunita gets bored sitting at home all alone. Once Sukanta goes to office in the morning, he returns only late in the evening. Does he ever care for house hold matters? Always he worries for his office. So many times Sunita reminded him to shift out of this house. But, Sukanta counters her under many a pretext, 'such a tiny township that one scarcely gets another option. It's luck to find at least this one. Besides, this one is well placed, not far off my office, close to the market place, hospital and bus-stand and in the vicinity of Bubun's school. We may not get such a favourable place. Tell me, what troubles you here? If it is the surrounding, then keep the doors shut, right? Just adjust, as long as we stay here.'

Sunita knows that beseeching Sukanta is hardly of any use. Thus she continued rotting amidst the squeezing periphery and chronic troubles of the rented house.

That day, Bubun went out to play. The neighbouring child struck him in his head. Sunita didn't complain despite profuse bleeding.

It's not that Bubun is gentle by nature or he doesn't fight with any body. But it is normal for children to play, fight and make friends. Why should she worry so much on that account? But Sunita does worry, whenever Bubun goes out to play. Every time he goes out, he returns with some more trouble. Sometime he breaks his head, some day his teeth, still some other day if he strikes another boy, the whole neighbourhood pounces on him. They chase him to the house and quarrel with Sunita. They threaten, "Control your child or don't accuse us if we thrash him some day." Uncultured, savage brutes they are, it's useless talking to them. Sunita locks up Bubun inside. The poor child whimpers, screams, cries inside the four walls. None understands his helplessness.

Sunita wishes for a rented house at a proper place, good company for Bubun, right learning for him. Here in this wretched neighbourhood, he already has learnt hosts of vulgar words by heart. When he utters them, everyone grumble against Sunita. Who does she blame?

Bubun has grown up. It's not possible to restrict him to home under threat. He intends to play out. Unless allowed for a day, he reacts in a wild manner. At times he pleads, insists, weeps, creates a scene, throws and breaks things. How long can a child be thus kept confined?

One day, Sunita detained Bubun at home. She frightened him of ghosts and goblins, lest the child should sleep. She locked the door of the house. Bubun sat on the window sill and looked outside pitiably at other playing children. That night he was delirious. He called some of his friends by name, complained that, his mother doesn't permit him to move out.

Next day, Sunita invited some of his friends to home. She offered them food and toys and asked them to come over everyday to play there. She also promised to feed them everyday. Then she went into the kitchen. She checked once and found Bubun playing happily. Humming in an undertone Sunita went into the bed room. After putting the room to order she returned to find Bubun sullen. He had broken all the toys out of anger and all his friends gone off after eating the food. Bubun was left all alone. He needed friends, he needed to play, he needed free air under the open sky, and he needed an open space.

Sukanta urged upon her to let Bubun go out, 'let him play. How long can you restrain him tied up to the end of your saree? Bubun is no more a kid. Unless he makes friends out of home, how can he learn the social systems?' But Sunita doesn't understand all these philosophy. She doesn't appreciate her child playing on dung pits with naked children secreting mucus from nose. Besides, she cannot tolerate Bubun being beaten by any of them and enter a quarrel when he touches any boy. Why should she endure with the complain and vulgar language of the whole neighbourhood and crush her head against the walls behind closed doors in solitude? Why should she thrash her own child to relieve herself of her anger? And why Bubun will promise to not go outside, only to sneak out the very next day, with all his toys tucked under his arm?

One day, Bubun was asleep. Sukanta was in his office. Sunita, after finishing her domestic chores was relaxing, looking out of the window. A dung pit was near by. Over it grew up a date palm tree. Over the tree two birds were playing the whole afternoon. Picking straw and grass from the ground, they flew up the tree. After sometime again they flew down. Even they held some discussion through their chirps. Sunita was engrossed with them for long three hours. Slow but steadily a nest started dangling from a bough of the date palm tree. Amazing! She thought. Sunita stayed rapt with wonder, until Bubun got up.

That day, on return from office, finding Sunita in a pensive mood, Sukanta enquired the cause. Sunita said nothing. She only wept.

Sukanta could not follow the meaning of such mewl.

Henceforth, every night Sunita had the same dream - two weaver birds weaving a nest on the date palm tree. She, though failed to decode the meaning of the dream, it obsessed her and day by day dismayed her. At intervals, Sunita had a dream that she herself is flying up the date palm tree and weaving a nest. Her home is dangling from a bough of the date palm tree and on its veranda, Bubun is playing. Here comes a strong wind. Tosses the nest. It seems a gale is approaching. Sunita is shouting at Sukanta to hold Bubun. The date palm tree sways so hard that Sunita wakes up startled.

Sunita these days stayed depressed. Sukanta failed to detect the cause of her sorrow. Everyday Sunita stood near the window and shed copious tears looking at the date palm tree.

That day, Sukanta came home around two o'clock for lunch. As he searched for Sunita, he found her at the window. She had failed even to notice his arrival. He went up to her. Standing next to her, he tried to find out what exactly beyond the window attracted her so much.

Now, the scene allured him too. A nest dangled from the date palm tree. One bird perched on it, the other one teaching the chicks techniques of flight. Failing to fly one fledgling drop to the ground. The bird flew down to pick it up with his beak. Tears roll down the cheeks of Sunita.

Sukanta touches the shoulder of Sunita softly. Sunita turning around falls on the bosom of Sukanta. Pointing a finger beyond the window, she adjures Sukanta with overwhelming sobs, "My Bubun needs such a nest, where he can play happily, roam about and dance freely. Sukanta, my Bubun also needs a bit of open sky and an open space."

CHAPTER FOUR

House warming

Sunita had a dream that soon after her marriage, she will build a house. In the backdrop of such a dream there lies a story.

Sunita's father was a government employee. Every one or two years, he was transferred to a new place. Throughout his service period, he must have changed some forty houses. Since the day Sunita remembers, her father must have changed at least twenty towns. Every time they faced the same trouble - packing of all the house hold items, discarding some as useless, then unpacking at the new place and arranging everything in order. The whole process was truly cumbersome.

But they were helpless as they didn't have a house of their own. The place, that was considered to be the birth place of her father, was a distant rural area, unapproachable due to lack of communication and the place that was considered a house, had flattened to ground due to lack of use over years. Her mother all along cursed her father that, had he had a house, the family would not be suffering like this. "It's only for the education of the children that I am running from pillar to post along with them," her mother used to say.

Her father, through out his life repented for this. Her mother, through out her life was annoyed with him. In spite of her mother's insistence, her father found no time to build up a house. Her father was an honest and sincere government employee. Is this why he could not achieve any thing in his life?

That is the very reason why Sunita was obsessed with having a house as soon as she got married.

On the very first night of their marriage, when Sunil reminded her to claim a thing as a mark of her victory in the ceremonial bet, which she had deferred then for a later time, unfalteringly Sunita asked him, to build her a house in an urban place. Sunil took the matter casually and said, "Just a house? Wait, I will build you such a house that will dazzle the eyes of the onlookers. Everyone will surely wonder about the house owner."

It was sufficient to pacify poor Sunita. Still, occasionally she did enquire with Sunil, "What happened to our house? How far did the matter proceed? Did you arrange a plot?"

Replies Sunil, "Is it so easy to find a plot in a township? Have patience. We have to be cautious about the location. So, I am in no hurry. The location should be proper for a house because, ultimately we will live there. A good society has to be there or the children will be spoiled."

Poor Sunil, no doubt he pacifies Sunita but he fails to convince himself as to how can he build up a house. Is it easy to build a house these days? What savings he has that he can erect a house in a flash?

Poor fellow Sunil, as soon as he joined his job, he got tangled in domestic matters. First of all, he repaid his father's loans. Then he married his two sisters off. Then followed the education of his brothers. But that was not the end of the burden, his own marriage ensued. The burden went on increasing after his marriage. Expenditure bloated. He had to go for a house on rent at his place of work and his salary was meagre for his maintenance. How much did he get to save some out of it?

On the other hand, all his friends already built up their houses. They didn't have to bear a burden of their families like Sunil had to. Long before they had purchased plots at cheaper rates. Of course they did persuade Sunil to go for a piece then. But, those days these things had not crept into his mind. He could not even conceive that, the price of plots will go up so fast. Besides the family burden was so enormous that he could not save a *paisa*. Thus he did not consider buying a plot. The marriage of sisters and education of brothers were primary for him. Thus at the end of this long wait, he was in such a state that, even if he wished to buy a plot, he did not have money. And the price had multiplied ten to fifteen times. When he thinks of a plot, poor Sunil only repents.

These days Sunil worries only for a plot. He is even saving a bit. At times he discusses with Sunita, "See, the way we are managing our life, I don't think we can ever build a house. We have to curtail our expenses. We have to be extra careful. Now you can take up the responsibility, I cannot manage the show. You know, I am a bit spendthrift," Sunita agrees. At times she too gets annoyed with him, "What did you do till date? Your service is about to end. Why didn't you consider of it earlier? Are the austerity measures only for me?" Sunita wishes to speak more. But she restrains herself. Because, she knew that it's futile to blame Sunil. He won't mend his ways. She feels forlorn. How cheerfully her friends are not leading their life? All of them have a house of their own. On meeting Sunita, they talk of their houses only; where did they built, how much they had saved, how much they spent, how much loans they arranged, how nicely the house is planned and even welcome Sunita for a visit. Sunita feels as if no one now invites her out of affection, the intention is only to show off their building, fridge, TV., car, washing machine at al.. Sunita covets not a single item of any of her friends except the house. Thus, these days she has stopped visiting any of them.

The austerity measures planned by Sunil fall flat. It's impossible to reduce expenses from any quarter. In this time of high inflation, how much one can save by controlled expenditure? Besides one has to maintain a minimum standard. Sunil makes an account, house rent five hundred rupees, petrol expenses at least a hundred, three hundred for milk, and a hundred for domestic help, all add to make a thousand rupees fixed for every month. Out of it, he can reduce a hundred out of the milk expenses. The house rent may reduce a bit if they shift elsewhere but below five hundred rupees, no good house will be available. With regard to ration like Dal, Rice, Oil, Salt, Vegetables and medicines one cannot compromise as that won't make much difference. Besides it is a habit with Sunita to buy some or other household items every month; she cannot manage without them, one month if it is door screens, next month it is bed sheets and still next month it is dress material for the child. Spending a sum after her saree or bangle or gold or some other essential things is a habit with Sunita which are out of their monthly budget. Sunil, a lecturer of Economics thus drags on with a deficit budget. The practices fail all his bookish theories.

Sunil, for all these, at times blames his luck. Had he had a job in some bank, at least with some amount of loans, he could solve a number of issues. But, bank job was out of his luck. Because of the precarious state of his family, soon after passing B.A., he joined the village school as a teacher. The school was newly established. As a local boy he got so much engrossed in the school affairs that he didn't find time to appear any competitive exams. The few he faced, he failed to get through, because of lack of preparation. But many of his friends of urban area got nice jobs. Later on Sunil appeared M.A. privately. The village school did not receive any Government aid. So, he joined a newly opened private college in a nearby town which got Government aid after ten more years. Of late only his salary seems a bit respectable. Still, ten years back he could meet his ends with a nominal salary but now despite a handsome amount he fails to do so. Everything has changed in the last ten years. Prices have reached sky high. That's why Sunil fails to buy a plot now.

Of late, whomever he meets, Sunil asks to arrange for him a plot. As soon as he gets a trace of information, post haste he runs to verify it. While one piece doesn't appeal him, another piece is beyond his affordability. Gradually Sunil is wearing out and squeezing his choice. When he proceeds to buy one wherever available, he finds all his pre-rejected plots sold out. Poor fellow, Sunil breaks down. Occasionally these days often he has wild dreams regarding the plot. He is even delirious. As he wakes up in the morning, he decides to stop searching for plots. He thinks, it will come if it is in his luck. Still with the slightest news, he runs to see another plot.

Suddenly one day one of his friends approaching him informs that he has got a good plot for Sunil. Adjacent to it, he himself is buying ten decimals. The location has future prospects. Though a bit distant from the town, within next few years, the township will expand in that direction. A rumour is spreading that a good number of official quarters will come up nearby. So, many a respectable family are buying plots there. "See Sunil, miss not this chance or surely you will repent. Very soon the price will multiply manifold."

Immediately Sunil ran to have a look of the plot. A plain patch of land beside the road, a bit low, though not declivitous. Sunil thought, 'not bad'. He showed it to Sunita as well. They decided to buy it by any means, the rest they will see while building the house.

The patch was divided into plots measuring ten decimals each, costing five thousand rupees per decimal. Sunil now concentrated on arrangement of funds. He had a saving of ten thousand rupees. The provident fund will provide twenty five thousand rupees. But the rest fifteen thousand was the real headache. Sunita proposed to pawn her jewellery in the bank to which, Sunil did not agree initially. But he had no option. So he went for it and the bank financed ten thousand rupees. For the rest five thousand, Sunita pushed Sunil to go for a hand loan from some friend. "Won't we pay back," she said.

Painstakingly Sunil did that too. Over and above, the cost of registration was to be met with. Somehow Sunil managed that too and succeeded in buying out a plot. A house can be built up, some time later.

Sunita knew that, if she sat silent, Sunil will surely squander ten more years. Had she not pestered him so much, would he have purchased the plot at all? So she warned him, "Why do you idle? Go and make a plan for the house first of all."

"What is the use of a plan so early? I don't have money. First I have to arrange that. How long does it take to make a plan?" Said Sunil.

"You cannot do anything. I'll arrange money. First of all, you go for a plan." Pleaded Sunita.

Thus, a year passed in making a plan. What appealed to Sunil, Sunita scraped. What appealed to Sunita was expensive, so Sunil rejected. Ultimately they agreed upon a point, conceding a bit to each other and finalised upon a plan. In the mean time Sunil had met some of his friends in bank and hashed out a house building loan. With the help of the loan from bank, some savings and a few amounts of hand loans, Sunil finally could build up a house.

On the evening of house warming ceremony, once the event was over, Sunil asked Sunita, "Are you happy now? See, how the house has been built to your taste. Now tell me, when shall we move in here?"

Sunita said, "First calculate, how much amount will be deducted from your monthly salary."

Sunil detailed out, "Five hundred towards provident fund, twelve hundred towards housing loan, five hundred towards thrift fund from which twenty thousand has been collected and five hundred towards the gold loan. Besides all the hand loans like, ten thousand rupees of your brother, five thousand rupees of my friend, five thousand rupees of the hardware store, three thousand outstanding of the electric store, two thousand rupees due to the furniture store. Excluding all these, smaller amounts add up to some ten thousand rupees. Moreover, construction of drain, colour of the doors and plastering of the boundary wall are pending."

Sunita said, "Do we really need such a big house? We will lease it out on rent. At least we can have a thousand and five hundred rupees per month. Let's first pay back the loans. After your retirement we can move in. I was worried as we didn't have a house. Whatever, we have a house now."

Sunil, adding up the loans in his mind concluded that, he might need ten more years after his retirement, to clear out the whole loan. This is their first house warming and probably their last celebration of moving into this house.

Lying on the floor, Sunil was looking vacantly at the white washed ceiling. Over the clean white wall, from somewhere ran up a fat house lizard and caught hold of the hopper.

CHAPTER FIVE

Abhimanyu in Chakravyuha

From the womb of his mother, Abhimanyu knew the art of entering the *Chakravyuha* and the skill of fighting the Seven Great Warriors as, much before his birth the *Chakravyuha* had been arrayed for him. Abhimanyu was the eldest son of the family. The death of his father at an early age made him a responsible chap. Along with his education, he looked after farming and affairs of home as well. He didn't have the opportunity to study further, after completion of matriculation in the nearby village school. Because, there was no college nearby. And as the financial condition of the family didn't permit him for staying at a hostel in some distant town for studies; after matriculation, ceasing his studies Abhimanyu focused on farming.

As a few years passed, a pressure built up on him for marriage due to the falling health of his mother and Abhimanyu was at a loss. At this very hour, spread a rumour that a college is coming up in the nearby town. Under the pretext of further studies Abhimanyu could avert the marriage proposals.

In fact, a college came up and a pair of wings as if cropped up on the flanks of Abhimanyu. He repaired his old bicycle and sold off a few bags of paddy to meet the cost of admission. He readied a pair of trousers and shirts. Within the last five years of wretched farm life, Abhimanyu had grown old prematurely. But, the first day he stepped in to the college, he felt as if his age came down by five years at least. Everything seemed new to him. Abhimanyu truly became happy and concentrated on his studies so attentively that, he secured seventh position in the entire university. It was a rare feat for the college and the locality and Abhimanyu caught attention of everyone. By the first day of B.A. class, he was already a star, as if a cricketer who secured six wickets in an over or scored a century by consecutive boundaries.

So, it was but natural for Sanghamitra one of his classmates to approach him for notes. Under the pretext of notes, meeting Abhimanyu, sharing tea in the college canteen, hanging out over the lawn, sitting next to him in the classroom and kissing his hand in the jungle during college picnic, though seem unnatural, in reality happened and Abhimanyu didn't delay to assume all these signs of love. Gradually, letters of love and poems exchanged hands through notes and books and Abhimanyu, focussed on reading Sanghamitra more than his class course. The more he studied her the newer she appeared. And Abhimanyu wasted all his precious time rote learning this new course.

Abhimanyu was in his village when the final result of his B.A. exams came out. He had never anticipated for a second class honours. He was least concerned for what others thought about him but he was worried for what Sanghamitra would be thinking of him, how sorry she must be for him. Around this time, he got a letter from Sanghamitra.

"Dear Abhimanyu, I felt sorry as I came to know about your result. The news might hurt you that my marriage has been fixed up with an engineer. The matter was settled so quickly that, I found no time to intimate you. Neither have I had the courage to inform about us to my family. Besides, had you got a first class first degree, I could have deferred my marriage by giving the news to my family. I am not much hopeful about your future with a second class degree. If my dad comes to know, surely he will be mad with me. So please don't mind. You will always be in my memory. Truly Sanghamitra."

Abhimanyu could not understand if he should be sorry or angry. But he realised that Sanghamitra was damn selfish who could make a scapegoat of his love for an engineer.

His mother's health was beyond recoupment. So, under the insistence of his maternal uncle, during the summer of that year, he married a girl of a nearby village.

Days passed on happily. Everything was new for him. He forgot Sanghamitra. Soon came up the concern for maintenance of family and money.

Abhimanyu appeared a few interviews. Failing in each of them one after the other, he arranged a few village children for tuition. After a few days, at the recommendation of the local MLA, he got a job of accounts keeper in a private factory.

Even though the job was no way remarkable still it was not that bad. At least it yielded enough to solve his financial trouble. Even after the day to day expenses he could save a bit for future.

The farm had provided him a quarter but there was no fixed duty hour as it was a private company. Even though he signed for ten to five working hour on the attendance register, once he went to office, his return time was not fixed. Some times he returned home not before nine or ten o'clock in the night and on some days he went to open the office at seven in the morning.

Abhimanyu was a responsible man and attended to his jobs very honestly. Besides, he had a list of each and every items of the factory, at the tip of his tongue. So, since the day he joined, the company went on making more and more profits. No doubt, his post was that of only an accounts keeper but he looked into the loss and profit of the company more and saved a good amount of unnecessary office expenses. Thus, the managing director of the company, was highly pleased with him and in one of the meetings of the board of directors, proposed for his promotion from accounts keeper to manager planning. As per the resolution, Abhimanyu worked as manager planning and because of his exceptional ability, earned the reputation of a deft administrator. But, at the same time he incurred the envy and jealousy of many of his colleagues. Unconcerned, he concentrated more on the profit and smooth running of the company. Gradually peculation and misappropriation in many fields stopped. He took successful measures to stop pillage of raw materials during transportation, supply of lower quality raw materials at the price of superior quality and sale of spurious products in the market under the brand of the company.

He devoted so much of time for the company that, he as if forgot his home. In the mean time his son had failed twice in college exams and sitting at home idle. Two marriage proposals of his daughter had foiled. His share of farm land in the village had been encroached upon by his cousins. His ailing mother had died. Yet he never neglected his duty and the company kept on tempting him with more and more offers.

Those who gained an unfair income, finding all their means choked, now started lobbying to remove Abhimanyu of their way. Their complains against Abhimanyu proved baseless on enquiry. The rumours which spread against him were rubbished by the company board. The company neither blamed him nor wished to blame him.

Having no other way out, the workers turned towards the union and activated it. Thus, for the first time over so many years, the factory ground to a halt for one day and four numbers of agitations were held under the pretence of arbitrary ways of the management. Their demand was, in spite of availability of many competent staffs, Abhimanyu's promotion without any test was illegal. So, removal of Abhimanyu from the post was their first demand. The management on the other hand didn't pay importance to the demand as it was a private company. But when the union obtained a stay order from the court the case headed for complicacy and the company, sought for a month's time from the union to take a decision on the fate matter and Abhimanyu was offered to stay on leave for a month.

Whole life, fighting with the Seven great warriors, when he was about to vanquish all of them, a time to lose everything started looming over him.

During this period of leave, for the first time by chance, after all these years, he met Sanghamitra. She informed that, she had been long deserted by her engineer husband and does repent for cheating Abhimanyu.

During this period of leave, for the first time Abhimanyu detects that his wife is bed ridden due to ailment. His elder son comes home drunk. His daughter is in some affairs with her classmate in college. His farmland in his village has been registered in the name of his cousins.

Abhimanyu, napping on his arm chair at the balcony of the company quarters, was looking back. What did he gain out of all these struggles? Is entering the *Chakravyuha* only the fate of the Abhimanyus? Do they really not know the way to get out?

Abhimanyu is dreaming now, as if the seven warriors well equipped in heavy arms and ammunitions preparing to ambush him jointly. Abhimanyu is shouting, 'it's not the rule of war. This is unethical practice.' Gradually they encircle Abhimanyu, who is sitting holding his head. He finds on the chest of each warrior written, Education,

Love, Service, Marriage, Money, Sickness and Death. Reflects Abhimanyu that I have won over each of them in every duel. But, it's impossible for one person to fight against their collective strength. Still Abhimanyu lifts his sword up, and his nap breaks with the jingling sound of a number of swords.

CHAPTER SIX

The uncanny mountain

Not far away from the town, a lofty mountain stood, which appeared blue from a distance though it was not really blue. It changed colour in every season and assumed distinct countenance on every different occasions. Thus since childhood it had crept into the mind of Amaresh that it was an eerie mountain. Countless concocted tales prevailed in his village with regard to the mountain, which since his childhood, Amaresh had heard from his friends. He had developed unconsciously a fascination for this mountain. Gradually as he and his friends grew up and as increased their engagements, they all drifted away from the mountain. Each of them got tangled in their ways and the mountain just wiped out of their minds.

Just a few days back, Amaresh came back to this town on transfer, from where the mountain near his village is clearly visible. It was a moonlit night when he opened up the window of the bed room of his rented house. A gush of air struck his face and somehow that mountain stood tall before his eyes. Thus it all started again.

He has seen this mountain since his childhood. Yet, never did he go near it. Many times he wished to go to the top and have a view all around. But his engagements kept him engrossed in such a way that he hardly found some free time for the mountain. And the guilt of failing to go near it hurt his conscience every day. Even he spent a few sleepless nights. And whenever he slept, he had awful dreams with regard to the mountain.

He consulted a doctor but, found not much relief. He didn't have any major physical health issue. He was just forty five, not much aged either. The doctor advised him to not be much concerned. It could be some temporary anxiety and absence of sleep could be due to some mental stress. He could consider sleeping peels for a few days. He could practise Yoga, go for morning and evening walks. He must keep the mind engaged. And worry not at all.

Amaresh knew where his problem lies. Still he was unable to solve it. He remains busy for the whole day since morning. Until he goes to bed he is fully engaged. But, before going to bed, as he opens up the window, the mountain would stand there mocking at him. And then his old trouble would start. He would smoke cigarettes one after other and remain awake through out the night.

Suddenly, one day while dozing off his arm chair he saw an unnatural scene over the mountain. No, he cannot any more check himself. An emotion erupted in his heart, a sigh added to that emotion, the sigh carried a load of discontent, a sort of revolt against the whole world. No one can stop his upraised step. All the bondages and shackles loosened over his feet, his hands got free. He bit off the rope with his teeth that dangled off his neck, threw off the hand cuffs on to the bed of his wife. Now he feels so relaxed. Now he could fly in the sky. No, no one can stop him now, after so many years, the mountain is hailing at him. "O my dear mountain! Wait, I am coming." Said Amaresh to himself and arose.

Amaresh was now just at the feet of the mountain. He looked at the top from below. No, it's neither very tall, nor blue, nor green, nor white, nor greyish. But, the mountain is a wonderful cocktail of all these colours. Someone is calling at him from the top of the mountain, "Come on dear friend, be not scared, we are all waiting for you here. It's an assembly of great joy and pleasure. Delay not."

Amaresh once looked at the mountain and once behind himself; no, there is no use in looking back any more. Forget the past Amaresh, that's all history, stories of corpses and cadavers when they were alive.

Amaresh approached nearer to the mountain and found wonderful steps leading up. He stepped on to the first step and slipped off. He was sceptical whether to go up or stay back. Again someone warned him from above, "Wait not, and think not, if you ponder, you may stick there like a statue of stone for ever. Wherever one paused to ponder, there only one stuck. Ponder not, come over, we are all here."

Amaresh again raised his feet up. This time he was a bit fast and succeeded. Then, one more step and still one more. He felt as if the mountain is receding. The strangeness of the mountain continued to bewilder him more and more. Can he back out any more, no he cannot back out. No, it's impossible for him to return. Painstakingly he has escaped once. Amaresh is taking step after step, the mountain receding on and on.

Next morning the hospital veranda was overcrowded. Amaresh Pattanaik has fallen off the rooftop. Amaresh Pattanaik, measuring five feet eight inches tall, lying unconscious on the hospital bed, his whole body from head to toe wrapped in white bandage, the oxygen pipe inserted in his mouth and saline infused into his arms.

Covered in white bandage, as if a snow clad mountain, his uncanny appearance resembles so close to last night's dream!!

Ladder

Cautiously I am climbing up rung after rung on the ladder. The man from above is warning repeatedly pointing at me a finger, "Don't climb man, you may fall down." (Shut up, I tell him in my mind, don't show off, in what way you are concerned, if I fall down?")

I am heading on and on very cleverly. In between, while resting a bit, I look behind. O God! So many I have overtaken? Behind me I find a queue, like a trail of ants, as if stampeding over each other. I try to recall a simile, apt for the scene but fail. The desire to rise up has overtaken me such that, amidst this uproar and confusion, I am looking up even though panting and gasping, 'How far up? Oh, the vision doesn't go beyond a limit, up, ahead, endless, countless number of steps. The riders too are no less. There is no space for even an ant. Everyone is helpless and hapless running carelessly helter-skelter.'

If I stand here like this, I may be overtaken, I may fall behind. Where is time to think over, amidst this jostling? Now it's time to run only. Wear out not, rest not, you might stick up there. Like the swarm of locust, they may take you over, they will march over you pushing you back and you would be reciting the couplets of *Gopabandhu*.

I again raise my feet up, by any means, I have to go. I have to join this mad race. What is so attractive there at the top of that ladder that one has to run? Do I have a fair idea on it? Or, am I running for the sake of running or, running out of fear not to be left behind? Am I also included in this race like the blinds like the insane?

The man from above is warning me, waving his hand dissuading me, "Don't proceed further", as if he wishes to say that, this race is futile, useless, there is nothing special here, it's all valueless, it's a vane race, everything is cooked up, illusion.

No. I am not ready to understand all these. Be there something or not, I will run. Did I come so far for no reason and shall I quit from here? What shall I do even if I turn back? Let there be nothing but, there is a charm in overtaking others in a race. Besides an unusual attraction has caught hold of me. No, I will not stop at the caution of any body, I will climb the ladder, definitely I will.

While climbing, after covering a certain distance I marked that no more it is possible to proceed further. What to speak of running, walking down is not possible. It is Impossible to stand even. The crowd is unruly, a jostling of panting, gasping and howling people. I wished to hold my head and searched for it. But it's impossible to move the hand up to the head. Now it is time to cow down, to crawl like an insect. Then only one might find a way further. Ahead of it there was no more jostling but it is only push and pull. Every one is busy pulling the other's leg. Only when one falls off another can rise up. No more it is possible. Better to retreat.

'O You! How can you turn back? Is there a way to back off?'

No more the words of the warner is audible to me. I know that behind me and ahead of me every one is as helpless as me. No, one more peculiar obstinacy is scraping my heart. I have to proceed on. I have to climb up all the rungs of the ladder. I can quit my humanity; the attachment of climbing this ladder is exclusive. Let whoever be before me, however intimate let one be to me, I have to pull their legs. Thus, I started pulling their legs. Flattening them out, I dashed on.

Now, just a few rungsare left before me along with warning of an invisible person, 'Proceed no more, there is nothing here, go back, you still have time.'

The last rung was to be stepped in. Before overflowing with the victory joy, I shout at the top of my voice, "O villain! Who is that, pulling at my leg!"

CHAPTER EIGHT

A city, once upon a time

After a long span of exile, I had directed my feet towards that town.

Covering a few mountains, jungles, rivers, streams, broken bridges, dark dirty garages, ash-coloured houses, shanty hotels, long electric wires, smoky chimneys, long railway tracks, worm and maggot infested drains, double and triple storeyed buildings, a few churches, mosques and temples, I reached a barren traffic crossroad. Roads led in different directions. A white marble statue, stood motionless at the centre. I approached it to ask something. I shook it. I suspected my fingers freezing, as I touched its ice cold body. Fearfully I stepped back.

Having no other choice, I opted for one road. Crossing over lane after lanes, crossroad after crossroads, bend after bends, I searched for many people. There wasn't a soul available. Even, the cawing or barking of crows or dogs was missing. A deafening silence loomed over the atmosphere. The whole town seemed dark by the shadows cast by casts of hawks roving the overcast sky.

Where did vanish all the people? Why this town is derelict? I went to a water tap. My throat was parched. But the water tap was also dry. Its hissing was as good as the panting of a tired snoring tiger.

After a good search, I located an old hotel. Carrying a lamp, a fellow came to take my order. I sat on the make shift bench and dozed off a bit. After a long time by the thudding sound of the tea glass on the wooden table, I startled up. I lit a cigarette. I sipped the tea in big gulps. As I stood to settle the bill, there was nobody at the bill counter. In fact, there was nobody in that hotel, nor there was fire in the hearth. I didn't find a single utensil like the pots, or pans, sauce pan, glass or a kettle. I was bewildered and ran away out of fear.

There was no way to go back from the town. The chirping sound of the cricket had made the atmosphere more dreadful. Even though, my heart shook out of fear, the earth below my feet swayed, an incessant urge to pee arose; with a stray hope to meet somebody, I was roaming across the town.

At different crossroads, garlands of rotten flower dangled from the neck of statues made out of skeletons. Rags, *chappals*, empty cartons of cigarette, condoms, soap, detergent, biscuits, and empty medicine wrappers filled the long deserted streets. Cobweb infested electric wires, scraped cars, heaps of torn tyres, empty garages, dried up trees and flowers in the parks, dusty nameplates of offices, milestones sunk deep into the soil, doors and windows closed and nameplates before houses seemed as if headstone over graves.

Seeing a silk cotton tree and a dug-well nearby, I remembered that once stood there the house of my dearest friend. I went near. Weeds and grass had overgrown around it. In the middle grew an anthill in the shape of a temple. Carefully I inserted my head into a window like opening. A buzzing sound came out of it. The spider webs stuck to my hair. The tail of a mouse or a house lizard as if poked into my ear. Widening the hole to accommodate myself, I jumped in. My friend was lying inside a coffin like box. He seemed to be delirious in his dream. I dragged him out of it. He got up. Opened his eyes. He greeted me with a half-hearted smile. He made me sit on a chair and asked about my well being. He went in and came back with a cup of tea.

While sipping tea, I asked about his wife and children.

He looked at my face in blank eyes. Probably he was unable to recognise me. Hurriedly he opened up a box. Searched out photos from an old album. Finding a number noted under a photo, he referred to a remark in a diary and said, "Gosh! Just see. Theses days I fail to recall any thing, recognise anybody. Where is time? Lots of botheration. Tell me, how are you? When did you come? When do you plan to leave? Where are you staying? What are you doing? Just see, I failed to make you out.

I asked him if he has got any news of the town.

"No dear, no. I don't go out much these days. I don't feel like going out. I don't know also, why no one comes around to meet me. It's after so many years that you have dropped in. So, how do I collect news about the town?"

"Don't you know anything? The whole town has turned to a sepulchre. All the houses have turned into graves. All the rooms to coffins. The residents have become cold cadavers. And you don't have any news? What are you all doing these days? Perhaps not a thing occurs here these days?"

"What difference does it make if a thing occurs or not? Oh! The friend exhaled a long sigh. Where is leisure these days? Fine, if something occurs or doesn't occur. See, I died while living my own life, while bearing my own burden and being tangled in illusion."

He stood before the mirror and plucking a bunch of grey hair from his head, placed on a plate. Then while counting them he said, "Did I consider any less about the town? And my hair turned grey due to overthinking about this town. The town never corrected. Hence, one day I locked my doors from outside and forgot about the town."

Standing before the mirror, he was chopping his elongated beards with the help of a bill-hook. I took leave of him and angrily rushed into the town. As I got tired due to continuous walking, I reclined against a tree to take some rest. Instantly two powerful hands tightly caught hold of my mouth. I shouted but not a sound escaped my throat. I struggled hard. Taking probably due pity, the hands freed me and asked, "Don't you recognise me?" My mouth had dried up due to fear. Did I pee as well? Still, boldly I looked at him. There was no tree behind me. It was an old man, as tall as a tree. My eyes were closing out of fear. The old man contracted himself and sat near me, "Are you scared? Don't you recognise me?"

I looked at the old man. Coarse grey hair. Curly eyebrows. A pair of shiny attractive eyes. Wrinkled skin. Slack muscles. And, a bunch of white hair on his chest. He wore a white dhoti, banyan and long shirt. A *tusser* shawl dangled from his shoulder. The old man was of tawny colour. He had long legs, hands, palm and a long nose. His tongue and teeth were seasoned with betel spittle. Gradually I recalled. The old man was once the heart of the town, as if the town itself.

Steadily the old man seemed normal to me.

I asked him, "Can you say something about the town? Here it self, there was once a blue town. It was happy, bustling and laughing. There was love, affection, attachment, birds were there, there were butterflies. Moonlit nights, blue roads and streets were there. Red singing birds flew in the blue sky. Waves of giggle and laughter overwhelmed everywhere."

He choked with sobs. Tear filled his eyes. He was looking with dreamy eyes at the distant horizon, perhaps in search of something. Again I asked him if he still remembers a thing about the town. The old man remained silent for sometime. Then he opened up his mouth. Heaved. Fumbling for words he said,

"Yes. Once it was a town. There were a few people. Keeping aside their own troubles, whole night they used to decorate this place. They were adding flowers on to the plants. They were colouring the sky. Scrubbing and polishing, they kept the moon bright and shiny. They were dispensing dreams freely for the eyes of people and love for their hearts. Once upon a time, such a town flourished here. Gradually, everyone started forgetting about the town. They indulged in envy and selfishness. They took only advantage of the town leading to conflict of interests, unwanted tussles, quarrels, fighting and bloody gang wars. Division on the basis of religion, sect, cast, neighbourhood and every possible type erupted. Walls of suspicion grew up between man and man. People feared to step out, even hated to come out. The whole town became desolate. Very soon the sky over the town darkened. The town became gloomy. For all times to come, people locked themselves to their houses and met their end."

"A few like me tried to drag them out, 'Come, let's try again, we will recover the lost smile on everyone's lips, we will join the broken hearts of all, make the flowers bloom again. Still there is time. But, no one paid a heed'."

"Since then I have been sitting here waiting for a living soul to share and be relieved of the burden of my heart. It's good that you have come back. The spark of life is not yet fully doused in the ashes of the cremation ground. Up till now, the throbs from the heart of some people are clearly audible to me, who wish to make life beautiful. It's good that you have come back. Search for that spark in the ashes. Light it, keep the flame high. And be sure, you will find faces emerging in that light. I do hear sound of a few worried steps walking beside the cremation ground, which disturb and distress me, but I fail to find their face. Call them near me or restore them to their life. May You have a trial; if by the magical touch of your hand, the town evolves again here, come to life, bustle about and overflow with laughter.

He then spewed out only hot vapour which made my body horripilate. A drop of blue light from his eyes splashed towards the sky. His whole body dazzled like lightening and turned red. Like a huge mountain he laid down facing up at the sky and breathed his last. A grave came over him with a headstone bearing his details at one end. I spread a handful of flowers over his tomb and sputtered to myself, "Again this town will be blue, the sky the moon and the ocean will be arranged in their respective places. The cadavers will resurrect. They will build up a ladder shouldering one another and climbing up at the sky, wipe out its darkness. They will smear the blue there. The sky will be blue. The ocean will swell with waves. Whistling zephyr will blow again. The birds will take off expanding their wings. They will sing, the sun will arise, the slumber of the town and its folks will snap. The streets will overwhelm with their laughter. Again a new town will come up, more beautiful than its previous version.

"Just wait. I am coming."

The unreal city

My transfer to that town was inevitable. Against my will, as I reached the main gate of the town, they asked me to sign a bond. The bond read, "I, during my stay in the town, will remain subdued to the chief of the town. His wishes will be my command. I will be bound to maintain the secrets of the town. I will be an offender to him, in case of the slightest negligence in this regard and will undergo the punishment prescribed by him." The dwellers of the town also gather at the carnival ground, once every year to take the same oath in the name of God, in the presence the chief of the town. The town followed Draconian laws. With the slightest discrepancy, immediately the authority exerts severest of punishments.

After having an idea, I no more had the desire to enter the town. I was scared, apprehensive of the occurrences in the town. Of course, before my transfer, I had got a hint on the place. But, reckoning with the advantage, disadvantage, incident, accident to be common to all the townships, I had laid least importance on the matter. Still, such harsh rules and regulations starting from the gate, was beyond my imagination.

I didn't have the guts to dishonour the transfer order as, it would mean dismissal from service. Expulsion from job would mean once again unemployment. After a long period of joblessness, on the recommendation of a well-wisher, I had availed myself of this job. Once this one is lost, there was hardly scope of getting another.

For the maintenance of my family, this job was badly essential for me. Thus, without a second thought, I signed the bond. 'So many people are residing in this town, so many others are coming here on transfer; what trouble would I face,' I consoled myself. To be frank, an unusual curiosity, despite intense fear was alluring me towards this strange town.

A permission letter was issued to me at the entrance of the gate on which, a message of caution was printed in bold letters - "Losing this card may mean death. Preserve carefully which is more valuable than your life." Producing the letter at the gate, I crossed the entrance. Two numbers of armed guards drove me in a vehicle to an address, where a well furnished house was waiting for me, dangling my nameplate before it. The guards retreated, saluting me. I entered the house and as was considering lying down a bit, the phone rang up. I picked up the phone. The chief congratulated me for reaching the town sans any trouble and wished me for a pleasant stay. He hung up before I could thank him. Lying down on the bed, I was thinking of the impeccable arrangements of the town.

The whole system was seemingly, though discordant to me as a new entrant to the town, the behaviour of the residents seemed natural and free from any special reaction. Like any other town here too, every one was busy in one's own way. No one was concerned for another. And I felt relieved of my undue fright for the town seeing their normal way of leading a life.

Gradually I started getting accustomed to the day to day affairs of the town. Even though certain unnatural incidents did occur frequently, the dwellers had learnt to accept them in the most natural fashion. Those incidents though made me reactive; I too forced myself to accept them in an usual manner. There was neither anyone to heed to my reaction nor along with expression of reaction, it was safe to dwell in the town.

That day, while heading for office in a bus, I saw a gang dashing into the bus and killing a man. No one turned at the victim despite his cry of distress. Even, his adjacent passenger was reading his book attentively as if glued to it. The bus too ran in a normal motion and the offenders got down at the next stoppage, like any other ordinary passengers. The cleaner of the bus threw the dead body out to the road and wiped out the stains on the seat with a piece of cloth. The passengers got back into the bus and occupied the seats unhesitatingly.

Another day, on the street, one person was tied to a post and some people who encircled him were stoning him. A few onlookers were clapping to encourage them. Still the passers-by proceeded on with least reaction. I paused at the scene. I could have asked them but before that someone shoved me off the place.

As I was unable to share my reaction with anybody, I was noting them down everyday on a diary. I, though wished to send letters to friends narrating the matter, I was scared to write them as there was a system of scrutiny of every incoming and outgoing letter.

While roaming, one day I reached a queer marketplace. It was named groom *bazar*. Males, exquisitely decorated were displayed in different stalls. Cards, displaying their price, along with name, address, educational qualification, age, profession and family background in short, dangled from their neck by strings. The fathers of eligible girls were coming there to purchase grooms as per their choice and affordability. Numerous such counters, displaying grooms were spread across the market. And, every type and standard of seekers could obtain a groom here. A few shops were even meant exclusively for the richer class, where a mention of fixed price was displayed. There was an option for bargain in a few shops. A few shops beside foot path, offered one price for every material. Some offered for discounts and at reduction price as well. While most of the shops offered ready-made items, a few displayed the board of order supplier displaying only a few samples. At the end of the market, there was a huge hall where auction sale was going on. There was a huge rush in this hall. Paying an entry fee of Rs.10/-, one could go in. A few platforms were there inside. A tidy groom was on the table and bidding for him was on. At the outset, someone came to announce a short bio data of the groom. A piquant speech on the nature and character of the groom was delivered. Then the bidding started from a few hundreds to thousands even to lacs. Fathers of the girls were choosing and bidding for candidates. There was a office on the spot to register their marriage if they wished. Or, the day, date, time were noted down for marriage. A few shops even sold second hand and third hand grooms and brides too. Roaming through the market for a whole day I returned to my house. That evening when I discussed the matter with my neighbour, with least astonishment he told me, "Look at my wife, can you ever imagine her to be a second-hand woman? I have come here for five years. You must have known how boring it is to stay here. What is there, before I leave the place, buyers will not be scarce if I go to sell her. Why don't you have one for yourself? How long can you eat in a hotel?" I could not sleep that night and spent whole of it with my diary.

There were very rich and influential men in the town. No rules applied in case of them. Out of them, a few were chosen for an assembly. The toughest and cunning most of them was declared the chief of the assembly. This chief and the assembly as a whole were considered the supreme authority of the town. There was an active system to communicate their decision. Any new decision was announced to the public by loud speaker every evening. Any changes in the existing rules were conveyed through distribution of leaflets. The public was bound to be aware of the changes in the rules. Because, any fault out of ignorance was considered equally a punishable offence.

The chief of the town had his clout through out the country. Thus, money flowed to the town unhindered. These members of assembly were so influential that, they could tweak the rules and regulation of the country as they wished. The dwellers stayed united and the chief enjoying that power had grown influential. The citizens had blind support for the policy decisions of the town. And the chief was so powerful that he considered himself as the supreme authority of the whole country. He, along with his gang had in his grip, the politics and economy of the country and used them to suit his wish and will. Thus, the people had since long forgotten the existence of a country outside the town and had assumed the town as the whole country. It was the only place in the entire country that was having an Oxygen mine and an artificial water making plant. So the whole country depended on the town for these two essential commodities. And, the country was unable to take any drastic step against the chief of this town. A powerful army along with ultramodern weapons was at the command of the chief. Thus the possibility of a war against the town was also out of question. As a result, the citizens accepted the decisions of the chief to be correct.

People were shot dead in broad day light. Plunder and abduction were common in the town. Fresh blood and sound of bullets on the street never perplexed the dwellers. They probably had long forgotten softer emotions like weeping, smiling, worrying, annoyance or anger. The town had long been independent from the country as no rule or regulation of the country applied here. The chief and his crew at times were scheming to take over the control of the country. Even they were preparing for a war against the country and accordingly keeping the dwellers apprised through various announcements.

In the mean time the chief came to learn the entry of a few secret agents into the town because his secret agents were well distributed through out the country. So, the law and order of the town hardened a bit more. Investigation, search and combing operations were conducted. Seventy persons were killed on suspicion within seven days. In front of my eyes, the head of our office was beheaded by a sword. He was under suspicion of the chief of the town, owing to his longer than usual leave.

Now, I was feeling unsafe to stay in the town. Considering my safety during this troublesome time, I applied for leave to go home. But, my leave application was rejected on the ground that no leave can be granted in this period of crises. I was requesting my head office through repeated telegrams for my transfer.

Meanwhile, countless murders and abductions had occurred through out the country. Holding this town responsible for all these mishaps, the country was considering for immediate measures. But, the chief of the town was still undeterred and defended all the mishaps before the head of the country as mere rumours. But one day, in a mysterious circumstance the abduction of a girl created a sensation in the country. At various places through out the country, defamation proposals were raised against the head of the country. In different towns, protest marches were held. And the head of the country was in no position to control the situation. The girl escaped the criminals tactfully and the real face of the chief of the town unmasked before everyone. The head of the country now decided to tackle this town by any means and suppressed the protests of other towns.

When the chief of the town was planning to control the whole country, the head of the country was planning to suppress this town. Now the army of the country surrounded the town with the standing order to bombard it in case of any adverse situation. The chief of the town, though was anxious, still he consoled the townsfolks that they have the ability to face the national army. Also, accusing a few citizens responsible for the situation, he was busy tracing them out.

The head of the nation threatened repeatedly to the chief of the town to surrender. When the general public was scared of bombardment, the chief of the town was consoling them not to be afraid of any bomb. Besides, they have sufficient secure places to save all. A constant announcement was on to keep the morals of the townsfolk high.

A good number of restrictions were imposed in the town. Search operations in many houses were conducted. The chief had announced that more than the outside enemy, the internal enemy were more detrimental and they must be finished up sooner than later. We have enough forces at the border to tackle the outside enemy. It's impossible for anyone to cross into the town. May the dwellers of the town enjoy their life here. Whatever it is, the chief of the town was indomitably courageous. The townsfolk had unshakable trust on his ability. Thus they had not lost their faith in him despite fear at heart.

At the day break of that night, I found the window of my house broken. I found a few papers along with my diary missing from my box. Even my permission paper to stay in the town too was lost. I intimated the head of my office in this regard. He asked me to remain silent. But, I was unable to remain silent. Because, the letter of permission to stay in the town was lost and non-production of papers is normal to lead to my execution. I applied to the head of my office and requested to send me a copy of it to the chief of the town who said that, I may be in greater trouble by confession. So I must remain silent.

Being disappointed from the head of my office, I reached to the office of the chief of the town to admit before him beforehand.

The chief was drinking a glass of fresh blood after his breakfast. Behind his chair, the geographical map of the town was beautifully decorated with a hundred and eight numbers of human skulls.

Stains of fresh blood dotted on his beard and moustache and around his lips which, he was licking off clean. He resembled a tiger who had just finished hunting. I dared not utter a word before him. He enquired me before I spoke out...

"Why did you come? There shouldn't be any trouble..."

I stammered, "theft..."

He roared with laughter. A few drops of blood sprayed over my white shirt. While I thought that my cleaning of blood with a handkerchief might offend him, he roared again,

"Theft in our land... something new..."

After a pause he said, "You can go through our records, there is no theft, no robbery, no plunder, no snatching, no rape, no murder, no land disputes, no dowry killing, no suicide, no unnatural death... no complain of anybody no protest on any thing and you come to complain of theft?"

The chief laughed so loudly that, his lever came out of his body. He swallowed it back carefully of course. Then he said, "Tell us if you have any other trouble. We may help. You are complaining of theft in our ideal town."

Mustering my courage I said, "I am telling the truth Sir. It's a case of theft. I am least worried for any other papers. But I worry for my letter of permission. Thus I thought it right to inform you from my side."

The chief now appeared serious, "OK, we'll see, if there is some mistake somewhere."

He pressed a switch. A television screen opened up before him.

An abstract of my stay in the town, since the day I came there, appeared. The chief was smiling at me. I felt like as if losing my senses.

When I opened my eyes, I was loaded with all my belongings on a jeep at the outer of the gate of the town. A letter of permission to leave the town was shoved into my hand where, the chief of the town had condoled my leaving the town, complemented my stay and cautioned me along with wishes for future. Another envelop contained my transfer order to my own town. A red bag contained all the looted items. I checked the bag. I learnt that my diary was not there. Still I put my signature to have received all the lost items.

My transfer order was a rebirth for me because no one has ever returned from this false town. Even these days I wonder at times, why did the chief of the town condone me rather than killing me?

I had opened up my heart in the diary during my tight-lipped stay in the false town which probably served for me as a boon.

Since I returned from the place, I never consciously thought of it and considering a nightmare, tried to forget it. Even these days at times, I find sensational news about the town on news papers. My heart pounds catching the headlines and I divert my eyes from the page.

CHAPTER TEN

A weird city

An office room inside a glass chamber. A table messed up with files. Two to three telephones and a pen stand, containing pens of different shape and size, an ash tray, *almirah* of various size and a buzzer on the table. Pressing a cigarette between his lips, pressing a receiver in his ear by his left hand, he was minutely looking into a file. I approached him in such a situation.

He neither shook a bit at the sound of my foot step nor paid a heed to me. I coughed twice. Still as if in a meditation, he was motionless.

'Sir! You should have asked me to sit down or wait for or get out. If not, at least you should have half-smiled at me out of courtesy. What is this?'

I wished to ask, "Are you dead Sir?" But, I got scared at such a thought of my own. Because, such lonely places, surroundings and silence often frighten me. It were as if an impregnable forest of those fairy tales, where drop of a pin sounds like an explosion. No one had seen me coming here. If Sir were really dead, I would be cross-examined first as the murderer.

Once again I looked at him intently. No. There was no physical movement at all. He was stagnant in the same pose up till now.

Intending to go back as I receded two steps, startling me, another telephone rang up. I felt as if, I should pick up the receiver myself and say, "Sir died just now. You may arrange for his funeral." But, the very next moment I thought, I will be considered the murderer. And, I was in no mood to be tangled in such mess. However, Sir moved to pick up the receiver, putting the previous one in place. He crushed the cigarette into the ash tray and said hello into the receiver.

I thought, it must be a ghost. Then I found him breathing normally. I thought, at least the man is alive. Finding him talking on the phone with a smile, I sat down before him on the chair and looked at him folding my hands. But he didn't look at me.

- Hello, yes, yes...

- Right, right...

- Very sad...

- I too think alike...

- People must die...

- How many died, how many lost, who killed whom, where, when, torching of house or flood...

- Terrorist

- Done right.

- They should be hanged.

- What about us? Are our people safe?

- How much wheat costs?

- How many *Chapattis* do they get?

- Half a piece? Good. The economy of the country did progress. May none complain of starvation.

- All the borders are well-guarded.

- OK, I am arranging.

- How many bombs were manufactured today? How many rockets? How many satellites were sent off? Right, we will see to it.

- Are all the files OK? Very good.

- Maintain a proper account of the number of births and deaths.

-No, no, no more for today. You cannot permit any one's birth for today. The figures of accounts may go topsy-turvy. No. Not even she. Tell her to bear after seven days.

- OK then.

I understood not a bit of the conversation. A table calendar lay on the table. I was leafing through it. A few dates were deleted by blots of black ink, a few were cross-marked, yet just a few were tick marked. As I was thinking to go through the news paper lying by, I was startled by a roar of laughter. Perhaps, Sir was laughing. The conversation was not yet finished, rather it was picking up intimacy.

I concentrated on the news paper.

"For a month, if no children are born, if all the old people die and if all the young men and women come forward to commit suicide for the sake of the country, then only probably all the problems of the country would be solved."

"Workers of one party today have killed a few workers of another party. No problem would be solved unless there is a tussle between groups on the basis of caste, religion or race."

"Many people these days prefer to be unemployed because of the perks doled out to the unemployed."

"To save the country from population explosion, people should come forward for foeticide."

"Honoured with the highest award of the nation for warding off a lac of infants seeing light of the day."

Reading the headlines, I put the news paper aside in its place. Even though I had been totally irritated, I looked at him being determined to convey my point before leaving. But, Sir was still busy. Perhaps, he was talking to else one now. Perhaps, some Sir of a different country.

- How is the climate around your country?

- Whether all the crops have been damaged or not?

- However, our country is much ahead in this respect.

- We have checked water by building a number of check dams. Who can apprehend in advance? Thus we are prepared in advance.

- What did you say? You can control rain? Where ever you wish, it will rain there? Rain stops if you don't wish? *Wao!* It's truly wonderful. Why don't you share the 'mantra' With us? When? Make it fast. I am sending someone within a day or two. OK, alright.

- The pith of the matter is that, you know our people. They are a queer type. It's the land of magic, Sir, one who knows to wield the magic wand, the land belongs to him.

- O yes, at least, the people can be regained, their trust can be revived. The situation now is a disaster. You know...

- OK, I will send.

- How much do you need?

- It's all yours Sir...

- Our neighbours are creating disturbances. Take a bit care of them.

- It's all your kindness.

- Your cows eat them?

- No, no. No need to worry. As it is, folks are starving in our country. It's alright.

- Where do we have time for war, Sir? Our internal feud is so high that, we cannot hear the challenges from outside.

- Still, if you wish, do send.

- You want the money in advance? It's OK. No. We too have produced enough. Enough to kill half of the wold. Still you can send fifty more.

- Now there is a bit of peace. Besides, unless people fight amongst themselves, it's a problem for us. This is one of our strategies.

- A lot to learn Sir. Why don't you send? Send just two persons. We can make them experts, within a month.

It was really boring for me. Still I was undone. I was adamant. I will speak, and then only I will leave. But, Sir had no leisure to attend to me. He was picking up phones one after the other and talking into them. Running such a huge country through two or three phones was amazing me and I was bowing before his extraordinary intelligence.

Sir was not looking towards me. I cannot of course say, if he had looked at me while I was not looking at him. A bunch of letters and other papers lay scattered on the table and I felt bound by my responsibility to arrange them in proper order. After staking them in one place, I picked up one to go through.

"We are performing as per your direction. Theft, robbery and rapes are on right track. Last night we have destroyed one village by torching it. We are inspired by your ideals Sir. I clearly remember the secrets you told me at the time of my induction to the party as a member. If one person cannot kill at least one person everyday, then the progress of the country is not possible. Only of late, I understand the essence of your advice. Our group is very active here. He has sent at least a thousand people up. All were traitors. Just one person of that type is a danger for the nation, a threat for us, and a hindrance to progress. The riots are perfectly being staged here. Your agenda is being executed in the right spirit. We fan it up when it cools off a little bit. May you relax!"

I got enraged. I looked at Sir with fear. He had detected me reading the letter and was staring at me with fixed burning eyes. He pushed a red button. With a roaring sound, two doors opened up at two sides of the room. Two robust body guards came out of the doors and dragged me. I shouted, "I have to tell you something important Sir. It's urgent. I have been waiting since long." However my throat had dried up. Not a word escapes it. They pushed me from the veranda of the glass house and returned back with a roar of laughter. The door of the glass house closed. A siren blew out. A red light flickered. I looked outside. It was already evening. Only a single star was shining and jet black darkness was approaching.

I reached my small cabin and poured two buckets of water on my head. Still I didn't feel relieved. I filled the bath tub and jumped into it naked. And under the shower I meditated on Archimedes for a long time.

Sitting on my study table, I leafed through Carl Marx. Then I opened up a history book and read about *Mohammad Bin Tughluq*. Hopping over to the Mughal era, I looked into the photograph of *Nur Jehan* and recorded the causes of decline of the Mughals. *Wao!* The history of this country is truly wonderful. All along the same rule 'Might is right' reigns here. So many rulers came, so many perished, so many will come again, so many now exist, who keeps an account of whom? But, an administration is there, a throne is there, only a change of the emperors. Rules change with emperors to suit changing times. When the change is implemented, lifestyle of the people has also changed. The people have also become very strange. Still, the country has a glorious tradition. I felt proud to have stepped into such a country. To know more about this land, I realised that I needed to toil more. Accordingly, as I planned out and arranged books in the shelf, I looked at the first window. As I opened it, my parents, my siblings, came up running through it. They loved me, caressed and fondled me. My father consoled me, mother wept before me and the siblings enquired as to why am I doing such a work.

Father said, "You have spoiled your life being involved in useless jobs. You spoiled such nice high education. What do you get by staying in this country? Let's go back to our own land. Don't you have a bit of affection for your own country, own village, own soil? Besides, how long we can toil like this. We have grown old. It's your responsibility to look after the family affairs. There is still time. Our Government is prepared to condone you. We have approached on your behalf. The Government will be pleased to lift your banishment order. Just, you need to beg an excuse. You do that, how long can you lead such a vagrant life?"

I answered, "I have not done any wrong. So, I cannot beg for any one's pardon. This whole world is mine. I can stay any where I like. Writing or telling the truth is no crime. Whatever I did there, here too I am doing the same. It's a beautiful country. There is a lot here to know. You may leave *Bāpā*! Allow me to lead a life of my own."

The window closed with the tears of my mother and all of them faded out. For sometime, I felt hurt. I wished to accompany them. But the very next moment, duty shrouded my emotion.

I looked at the second window.

As it opened, the whole atmosphere was filled with a sweet fragrance. A girl, draped in a red saree walked up to me tinkling her feet and dangled from my neck. Kissing me she asked, how long, how long more my dear, when will end your banishment, when will arrive for us that golden morn? I caressed her head, her back, and her tangled hair and cursed the time. I indicated her to sit, brooded over the past for some time and sighed.

At least, you didn't deserve this injustice my dear! Why at all did you love a man like me and welcomed troubles. What you got, O what did you get, only unnecessarily you were harassed. Still there is time, go back, lead a peaceful life, enjoy a family. Go on, I absolve you of the curse of my love.

No. I have come prepared. I will stay with you, wherever you stay. I will share your life. I will work for you. I am your love. I cannot live in a land where you don't stay.

One day your Government will realise. It will accept me. It will ask the prodigal son to return back. One day my world will surely recognise me. My people will surely welcome me. You wait for that day my dear. Allow me presently to lead a life of my own. I wish to learn more things about life.

She wept. With her tears closed the second window. She retreated. I felt very lonely. I felt a twitch in my heart. I made a cup of tea on the stove and deciding to skip the dinner I opened up my diary.

I face injustice everywhere. The folks, there and here, are all equal. They are always silent. Expert in enduring with injustice. I challenge injustice. I protest. I raise my voice. That's why I fail to lead a peaceful life. My beautiful world, my pleasant family, my love, everything is dwindling. I am counting my days here; waiting for the birth of such a person, whose birth will only relieve me of my responsibility.

That day I slept drooping over my diary and when I got up it was late. I finished up my morning routine, ate my breakfast and headed for Sir's office.

That day the town was jostling with crowd - as if some untoward incident had occurred. A number of grounds were noisy with speeches, some thing was being announced on the loud speaker.

A young bride had been burnt alive. A man had been shot dead on the street. Staff workers of various agencies had brought out protest march hoisting black flags.

The town was in a pother that day. It overflowed with 'Long live', 'Down! Down!', 'We want our demand fulfilled' protest cries. The police jeeps were rushing helter-skelter. The situation was uncontrollable, almost chaotic, as though the world is on the verge of a great deluge.

In such a situation I reached the glass house office. It was not easy this time to enter the office like any other time. The police forces were roving all around the office. Yet I was stubborn to enter the office. They warned me to stop or face death and asked me to come on some other day, but not today.

I said, "I have got important business. I have prior appointment. I showed them my appointment letter. Someone went in and came back. A sentry came to frisk me. There was nothing in my pocket except pen, paper, handkerchief, match sticks, coins and a piece of cigarette. Excepting the cigarette and match stick, they shoved the rest into my pocket and allowed me in.

The glass house appeared very dejected, as if there was none, nowhere. Still, a few unknown faces did appear, but receded murmuring a thing or two.

I expected, Sir must be very agitated as the town was almost boiling. But, there was no trace of any adverse emotion on his face. On the other hand he seemed overjoyed. He asked me to sit down, as soon as he saw me. I too was pleased with his mood and occupied a chair before him. As Sir was about to ask something, the phone rang... Hello...

: Yes, Speaking. I looked around. It was beyond my conception that any one else other than me could be there in. A number of Young men and women were silently working on various files and looking through magazines.

The conversation over telephone was picking up.

- What? A blind girl has been raped?

- Nothing to worry. Every girl is blind in love.

- Let there be procession. Let there be protest march. Let them shout slogans. Should these upset one?

- Hm.. OK... I am arranging.

- We wish for a mass awakening. We wish people to take to streets raising voice against injustice. Then only the situation of the country will change.

- He is a rogue. Put him in jail. Unnecessarily out of self interest, he is instigating people.

- Increase the bonus. Withdraw the procession. There is not much harm.

- No. Right now it's not possible. We are busy otherwise.

- OK. Bye. *Namaskar.*

Sir hung up the phone and looked at me. Before I introduced myself, unfalteringly he recited my name, village, family, heredity and the like in details along with my breakfast of this morning, how many times I peed.

I was stunned, a bit scared too and said, "Sir! Amazing, your intelligence system!

Sir smiled a bit and turned towards the girls. Sir probably doesn't like flattery, what I gathered.

The girls encircled behind his chair in such a manner that, he appeared as if the King *Vikramāditya,* sitting on his *Battish*

Singhāsan (The mythical throne, adorned by thirty-two female figurines) decorated with fairies. Floating a scented smile on her lips, each girl was as if waited for Sir's order.

Now Sir signalled at the young men who along with their files stood in front of him. Sir pressed a blue button. A spic suited man came up. Sir ordered him to take interview and concentrated on his file.

- Your name?

Sir getting upset said no need to ask anybody their name. Nothing works by a name. Besides, the nomenclature system of our land is also quite queer - bearer of the name *Bhim* could be thin and weakling, a *Jñāna Ranjan* could be a dullard, a *Gorāchānd* could be one jet black, a *Bīrakishor* could be a coward. All useless names, nothing works by a name, he grumbled and focused on his file.

- What can you do for us?

- Whatever you order Sir!

- We can extract that from you by any means. Of your own, using your own head, what can you do for us, for the country, for the public?

- My life is dedicated for the public Sir!

- Seems too good. It may so happen at times for you to compromise your self respect for the honour of the country. Can you manage that?

- I am ready to do everything for the country Sir!

- How do we believe? Remove your trousers. Can you do that?

- (The boy stammered) At least it's not essential now Sir!

- How do you know?

- I... my trousers... no Sir... I cannot do that.

- Get out of here. A coward like you cannot do any thing.

Thus carried on. One after the other. The interview continued endless.

The great majority of the fairies had withdrawn from behind Sir. Just one or two were left who hung from Sir's shoulder like bats. And Sir was busy with the scene.

Right at that time, a stark naked fellow came up before Sir and boldly announced, "I am ready to do any thing Sir."

Sir clapped being overjoyed, "Bravo! One honest fellow is enough for the country." He directed one girl to test the boy's potency.

It will be indecent to narrate what ensued. Even though we had closed our eyes, from the continuous prompting of Sir, we could guess whatever was going on.

Before the final reaction of Sir, I had left the room. While leaving the town, I realised probably by mistake, I had entered some weird town.

CHAPTER ELEVEN

A queer flower

It was wee hours as his dream broke. The man sat up on the bed rubbing his eyes. He felt strangely fresh. The house was filled with a sweet fragrance. Once or twice he dragged deep breaths and sniffed the aroma shutting his eyes. He got up from the bed slowly and sniffing the source, opened the window up. A whiff of sweet smell as if obtruded upon the room. He stood gazing at the back yard attentively. After sometime, he felt as if he was elated. Gradually the dream haunted him. An eight-handed, three headed man, as lofty as a mountain, eyes as big as wheels of a bicycle, neck lace glazing like twinkling bulbs, got down from the back of a bird in his backyard. Waking him up he said, "You only are my true devotee. I bless you. By tomorrow morning you will find your situation changed." As the man bowed before him, the whole region brightened up, as if by a bolt of lightening and the bird screeching in a horrific tone flew up into the sky like an aeroplane. That horrid sound of the bird, in fact had broken his slumber.

Smelling this sweet aroma since morning he pondered, 'could the dream come true?' Tracing the aroma he reached his own back yard and found the smell emanating from the dung pit. A queer fragrant flower bloomed on a plant on it. On the golden plant, buds resembling diamond have come up, blue hued flowers were as if like pearls. 'It has to be that strange plant, which is the boon of the God' he thought. He ran into his house and woke up his wife. His wife woke up startled and said, "How come you have turned so handsome?" The man had not yet marked. By now, his arms had grown strong and fleshy. His bony rib cage had grown muscular. The sunken belly was flat with flesh and fat. His dried up cheeks had become chubby and plump. He could not believe his changes and thought; it must be the grace of that smell.

"Get up. Let me show you something," he said to his wife. Both approached the plant. The woman also could not trust her eyes. The man narrated the dream to his wife. Happily, they bowed before the plant with reverence and indulged in their usual *poojā*.

After getting the plant though they felt as if they got everything, they were clueless as to what to do with the plant and how will their sorrows wipe out. His wife pestered him to recall what more the God had said to him. The man however failed to retrieve. Still, he could remember clearly that, adivine person came to offer him a boon. Thus they decided to not worry much on the matter as, it was His responsibility to take care of the matter, who has granted them the boon.

Since that day, the man appeared very joyful and frequented the town. He felt himself to be the greatest man of the town. The townsfolk too were astonished by these sudden changes of the man and started imagining things about him. Even a rumour spread that, 'he had retrieved some hidden treasure of his forefathers, or is engaged in some illicit activities. Be whatever, he has surely tumbled upon a fortune. If not, one who sought for help till yesterday, how could he be so careless today? Don't you mark the glaze on his face!'

The man or his wife, no more pondered on how to use the plant. But, the plant had become an object of worship for them. By now, clearing the dung pit, they built up a platform around it. Every morning and evening, they started worshipping under it.

Suddenly one day, news spread that, the richest man of the town is unwell. He has been struck by some incurable disease and all the physicians, quacks and even sorcerers have failed to cure him. Further news came that, he could die any time soon. The man came to know the matter. He lamented profusely as, once upon a time the rich man had helped him in need. So, let it be for once last time, the man decided to meet the rich man. His wife too felt sorry for the rich man and suggested, "What can we do for him? At the best, hand him over a piece of the fragrant flower, so that he may breathe his last peacefully."

Making his way through a jostling crowd, the man reached the rich man and asked, "Do you recognise me *hazoor*!" The dying man wavered for a bit and nodded. The man thought, how can he recognise him on his death bed? He however extended the flower at the rich man, "Keep it hazoor, under your pillow" and bowing before him he came away.

By the sweet smell of the flower, the rich man got up and sat on his bed. He felt as if he is recouping. He took the flower near his nostrils and dragged a whiff of the fragrance. He felt as if he recovered completely and joyfully ordered to search out the man. "I am going to give him all my belongings. This flower carries some divine power."

Gradually the news spread across the whole town that the man residing at the edge of the town, does know some magic. He owns a strange flower, inhaling whose smell a man can recover from death bed. The persons who knew a bit of him said that, he has tamed some goddess. A few said, they have seen him worshipping at late hours of night lighting fire at his back yard. A few were fearful of him, still a few sceptical of him.

Again rumours spread across the town. The incident came up on the news papers, narrating the strange flower, the recovery of the rich man and many an unnatural stories. Even a rumour spread that a dead has come alive. Gradually a crowd gathered before the house of the man. He didn't get rest from morning to evening. Everyone told him a painful story of one's own. The man offered them a smell of a petal of the flower or a leaf of the plant. Each felt benefitted out of it. Some recovered from illness, some issueless were blessed with children, some unemployed got jobs, some won over legal cases and still some passed exams because of carrying a flower in their pockets. Gradually the glory of the flower spread out and the man remained so much busy in distributing the flowers that, he got no time to think of any thing else. His wife and children were engaged in plucking the flowers, cutting and packing them in tiny packs. He soon became the most sought after person of the town.

Now, it was impossible for the man to make packets and distribute the magic flower all alone. So, he employed a few helpers and to meet their expenditure, he charged a price for each packet. Now the public no more faced trouble for the flower. They paid a price and collected a packet. Still there was no decline in the demand of the flower and the man could amass loads of wealth.

This huge earning with least labour became the eyesore of many in the town. A few came up to abuse him and spread various indecent rumours against him, like he is a fraud, no such magical plant existed in his garden, and the flower didn't have any such power. Even, some fell ill sniffing the flower and leaves distributed by him. Some have gone mad. Even a few unnatural deaths were cited to have been caused by the flower. They demanded that the man must be dissuaded from this practice as a safeguard measure to check further mishaps. The rush for flower however refused to dwindle from the man's door.

Day by day, the crowd grew so huge that, on certain days the flower and leaves of the plant exhausted and the seekers had to wait for the next harvest. Taking advantage of the situation, some cunning fellows collected the flower packets in advance and stocked them to sell at higher price in the market. The craze for the flower increased many fold as others too got an opportunity to earn an extra buck out of it. Thus there started a hubbub before the man's house. The libel mongers instigated the uproar and spread slander against the man. Gradually a law and order situation started there and on certain days, a cut finger, a clipped ear, a portion of nose and even a dead body was found laying. It was impossible on the part of the man to distribute the flower any more. He decided to discontinue it henceforth. And, one day he stopped.

As soon as the distribution of the flower stopped, the townsfolk became restless. A sort of turmoil started in the town. Again a rumour spread that the man is exporting the flower stealthily. A few protest march were held. But the man was unmoved. A few even proposed him to hand over the plant to them so that, they can arrange for the distribution. The man gave them a bit from the branch, root and even seed. But nowhere the plant grew up.

One day in the wee hours, a few people came in a chopper and got down in front of his house and asked, "Are you the owner of that magical plant?"

"Yes *hazoor*!" He replied.

They went near the plant and examined it with a number of equipment. They tested the soil, measured the height of the plant, length of the leaves and the length and breadth of the entire piece of the garden. They asked the man if he is educated or at least literate.

"No *hazoor*. I am illiterate."

"OK then. Come with us. We'll discuss the matter."

The man spread a mat on the floor. The fare, handsome tall men sat on it and discussed in an incomprehensible tongue amongst them and proposed, "See, this is no ordinary issue. We have conducted various tests in our laboratory. It is no ordinary plant. It is the 'Mrita Sañjivanī' plant that once existed and now is extinct from the surface of the earth. We have tried to plant it at different places. But it doesn't survive. The soil of your dung pit contains some extraordinary chemicals. Later on we will try to grow it in other places, after conducting other tests. But, it's essential for us to establish our laboratory and business centre here. Even if you disagree, we are compelled to acquire the piece of land on the basis of national interest. We have measured your garden. It's eight decimals. You may quote your price. Of course, later on we will be compelled to buy out the adjacent lands. If you wish, you can sell out your house also and shift elsewhere."

"I can part with everything hazoor, except with the plant," said the man.

"OK then," they said. "We will not take your house. If you wish, you can have the job of the gardener. You can see the plant everyday and take care of it as well. But thing is that, even if you deny, we are bound to buy your garden."

Finding no way out, the man agreed. They left, collecting a few papers signed by him towards the sale of the land.

After a few days, the construction work began there. High walls came up. Glass walls erected around the plant and the house of the man hid behind those walls.

These days, he enters the garden producing an identity card to a sentry at the gate. He waters the whole garden. Gets tired. Sweating from tip to toe, he sits beneath a tree and looks at the plant. Due to over work, his ribs have protruded. His jaw line has bulged out. But with a peculiar attachment, we carries on working for the plant. He wishes to approach the plant and caress it once. But, he lacks the permission to go near it.

One day he shouted at the door of the glass house, "The plant is mine. It has been forcibly snatched away from me." He banged the glass walls and shed copious tears. "I wish to fondle my plant once at least *hazoor*!"

Same day, the man was sacked from his job on the pretext that he has gone mad.

CHAPTER TWELVE

A day of leisure

After a long time, they were setting out on a trip. After a protracted debate in favour and against the trip, finally to go out they agreed. After the office hour of Dinesh, they will board the last bus and Dinesh will come back by morning to join his office. Ritu and Jiten will stay there for two more days.

Ritu, of course, urged upon Dinesh to take leave for five days. But Dinesh declined. He had planned to escape the trip feigning absence of leave. His plan was to join office for a day. The next day, due to a strike in office, he will spend relaxing, with none at home. He need not have to worry for anyone. He will be free to act as per his own wish. Thus, knowingly he had withdrawn from Ritu, the information of strike at office. Or, she would have forced Dinesh to take leave for a day or two.

Dinesh, on return from office, changed his dress hastily. By then, Ritu and Jiten were almost ready. Jiten was hurrying and pestering, "Dad, quick. Let's go to uncle's place."

Jiten is a three year old effing kid, difficult to manage. Once he gets in the bus, he would insist to drive the bus or threaten to get down. Ritu was yet to be done fully with her make up. She had a feeling that she has forgotten many things in hurry. Repeatedly she was checking herself before the mirror, at times straightening her saree, or searching in the dressing table drawer, or running at the *almirah*.

"Will you find out, where is my safety pin? I know, because of this boy, nothing remains in place and you, why do you idle? Why don't you help me a bit? You accuse me of delaying only."

"What can I do? Am I your make up man? How do I know, how many layers of powder would you smear, how much thick should your lip stick be, how many folds your saree should have, which blouse to match which saree?" Said Dinesh.

"Who asked you to be my make up man," snapped Ritu. "Don't you see all the things scattered? Can't you arrange them back? Can't you switch off the freeze? Clean the water bottle of the child and fill it. Put it in the bag. You get your luggage ready. Put out all the switches. So many jobs at hand, can I manage them all alone? And don't allege me if we fail to catch the bus."

Dinesh silently attended to the chores. He knew, any disagreement now may be dangerous. Ritu might refuse the trip upsetting all his plans.

Ritu loves her own home very much. Seldom does she step out easily. Dinesh pinches her at times, "Couldn't you please move out somewhere for a few days and allow me a leisurely, solitary day? See, so many of my works are pending. Being tangled with you people, I fail to attend to any of them."

Fences Ritu, "If you are getting bored, better you move out instead." Ritu, after marriage had wholly taken over the house from Dinesh. She occupied the house as if, it's she and Jiten or Jiten and she and Dinesh is just an auxiliary verb between them. Since three years, the same activities, the same life style, the same routine from dawn to dusk and Dinesh was fed up since a few days. He needed some change. He is as if tied to a post and meandering on a fixed orbit. He did need a change. Thus he impelled Ritu to attend this wedding function and reconciled her to his proposal. After a long gap, for the first time Ritu is going out, to attend the wedding ceremony of her fast friend. Thus, Dinesh is meekly cooperating her, may her mood not change and shatter his plans. Any how he has to catch the last bus.

It was late by the time they reached the wedding place. Everyone ran up to them seeing Ritu. After a long time she was there. "Where were you lost," a few girls led away Jiten and the lovely kid was lost in the crowd. Ritu got busy with others. Dinesh was left alone, all alone. He, somehow felt very light, as if escaped a dungeon after a long time, where someone had stuffed and locked him in. Else one now taking pity released him. Dinesh, leaving the crowd behind, came on to the street and his mind was comparing the transmuted town before his eyes, with the age old familiar town of his memory. The shops and market place are so overcrowded these days and he was unable to accept that he was reading here once upon a time.

'Would Ritu be worrying for him? Would Jiten be bugging others?' He returned back to the wedding place. The feasting had started. Jiten was eating with a few girls on a table. As soon as he saw Dinesh, he shouted showing a piece of meat at him, "Here Papa, we are eating *feast*". The girls giggled. Dinesh was relieved at the jape of Jiten, 'Seems, he doesn't miss me!' Ritu popped up from somewhere and asked Dinesh to eat something, "You didn't eat any thing since morning." Dinesh felt the joy of Ritu, 'Seems, she has been hosting the ceremony!'

"Ritu, don't worry for me. I have taken my food. Don't look for me any more. There is a friend nearby. He has invited me. I will stay for the night there. I will go away by early morning. Who knows where you would be taking rest in this crowd. Why to disturb others while searching for you? Thus, I will not meet you in the morning. I will straight leave from the friend's place. I have to reach office right on time. You just take care of Jiten."

"Don't worry for him," said Ritu. "So many are there to look after him. Don't you see, how happy he is here? He nettles because he gets bored at home. OK then. I will return after a day or two."

After dinner, whole night Dinesh wandered through out the town aimlessly. After a long time, he felt light and carefree. He was in no mood to waste his freedom. In the morning he returned by a bus and joined his office on time. A load of works awaited him there. So he could not go home. Besides, he didn't have any engagement at home. He was tired after the office hour and felt sleepy because of the previous sleepless night. So, he ate his dinner out and went back home. The office was off the next day. There was none to disturb him at home. So he planned to enjoy a long sleep and spend a leisurely day. Dinesh went to bed comfortably.

His slumber broke with a knock. He found it to be nine o'clock in the morning. At once Dinesh remembered that there was no one at home. That means, he could sleep a few hours more. No one to check him. There is strike in the office today but who is it knocking the door so early? Dinesh was adamant not to pay heed to it. But, he could guess the milkman from his "*Bābuji! Bābuji!*" call. Dinesh, perforce opened the door. But how to collect milk? He remembered the steel round pan where milk is stored, but he didn't find it. Thinking that any utensil can do, he came up with a bucket. The milkman laughed, "It's the trouble when *'no one'* is home."

Dinesh now thought, what would he do with so much of milk in absence of Jiten? Of course he needs a cup of tea, but if he keeps milk, he has to boil, store it carefully, wash the utensils, the cup and saucer, a real headache.

"You can give just a quarter today and don't come tomorrow." Dinesh collected the milk in a glass and put it on the dressing table. He decided to brush his teeth and make a cup of tea for himself.

When he went to the wash basin, he didn't find his toothbrush. He looked for it, from the drawing room to the bathroom but the thing was untraceable. He got irritated, "Why doesn't one put a thing in the right place?" When he decided to manage without toothbrush and searched for the toothpaste, he found it lying on a shelf, uncapped, squeezed out of the tube and a dead big black ant stuck to it. Dinesh thought, 'Leave it!' He went to the bathroom and washed his face and mouth. To make a cup of tea, he searched for the saucepan.

Day before yesterday, when they were leaving home for the trip, Ritu had made Dinesh a cup of tea. But, she left the saucepan soiled in a hurry. Had she poured a bit of water in it, it would have been different. Dinesh now found dry tea leaves sticking to the pan and an army of ant pouring on it. Dinesh threw it in the scullery and placed a bowl on the gas stove. He poured water into it and as went to get the glass of milk, he found a cat jumping off the dressing table. It had drunk the milk, overturned the glass by its tail, spilling the rest over the dressing table and soiling the floor. Dinesh, cursing the feline in the most obscene tongue, ran in search of a jute sack to soak the spilled milk. As he spread the gunny over the spilled milk, he remembered that, he had left tea boiling on the gas stove. At least he could have a cup of black tea. On reaching the stove, he found the tea over-boiled, thickened and as red as blood. Dinesh switched off the gas stove. No, he cannot manage these domestic chores. Rather, he should go out for tea. Besides, he needs a toothbrush also.

Dinesh put on his dress and headed for the tea stall. He ordered for a cup of tea and leafed through the news paper. Because of his engagements of late, he has failed to keep a track of the tidings. After a long gap as he flipped the news paper, he couldn't follow a single word of it. Leaving the news paper, he lighted a cigarette. A few friends came and teased him, "Oh Dinesh, how come you are relaxing today?" Dinesh smiled at them and felt happy that, he got some leisure after a long time. After he finished his tea, Dinesh wished to loaf around or read some books in the library. Or, should he switch on the TV and enjoy cricket? Or, drop in some friend's place! He even wished to go for a trip around the nearby woods. With so many thoughts thrusting into his mind and failing to decide upon one, he went to the nearby stationary store to purchase a toothbrush. He found a host of pens of new design displayed there. He checked each of them and selected one. Since so many days, he hadn't written a letter to any body. It was hard to find a pen at home as the child throws them hither and thither. At least Jiten is absent today to misplace this one.

Dinesh, on reaching home realised that, he has returned with a pen in lieu of a toothbrush. "Excessive freedom spoils man," he thought, "one should be a bit cautious." He appreciated his own new theory and planned to write a thesis on it, of course, as soon as he gets leisure. While brooding, what more to add to that thesis, he saw an old 'tooth-stick' *(Dānta kāthi)* which had been pushed into a hole as a toy for Jiten. Dinesh examined it, if it had dried up and hardened. But finding it alright, he soaked it in a bucket of water to soften. He felt it a chance. While chewing it, he was struck with another thesis, on chance and accident - role of chance and accident in life; to what extent luck is responsible and what is the percentage of action, whether action defines luck, or vice versa, or they conform to each other, or independent of each other? He split the tooth stick along the length and scraped up his tongue. As he washed his face, the thesis on luck and action wiped out of his mind. Now he was ravenous. He opened up the biscuit and *muḍhi* tins. Only a few crumbs were left there. Did they empty out of fear of spoiling or did it exhaust in normal course?

Dinesh opened up the freeze. A whiff of unbearable stink came out of it. It was switched off since the day they left. He switched it on and found a few vegetables rotting. A pool of water had gathered in it. He needs to clean all these now or, Ritu will shout at him on arrival. There was nothing edible there in the freeze. 'Let's clean it later' he thought and switched of the freeze. 'First I need some food.' Dinesh looked at the wall clock. It was noon. Why to have breakfast anymore, better to eat the lunch, he thought. He decided to have a bath first of all. 'Since long I have not bathed in the river, let me go there once' and he headed for the river, despite the searing heat. On the river bank, he washed his motorbike and got down into the river.

He found a bathing '*ghāṭ*' after walking on the hot sand. Sand bags had been aligned as a check-dam.

He turned back and found a trail of footprints he had left behind on the sand. It was a strange experience for Dinesh that, the footprints belong solely to him, none else. Is there any thing to be proud of it, he thought. Only I know that these footprints are mine. Can any one coming later identify them to be my footmarks? Do I have any thing uncommon to distinguish my footmarks from those of others? Such a peculiar philosophy of life captivated him. No one will remember him once he is dead. Has he done any thing notable? May be after a few moments, a whiff of wind will wipe out all his footprints. Dinesh repented, only by eating and sleeping a great life has gone in waste. Dinesh swam in the river. The sand below was visible through crystal clear water.

He climbed upon a boulder to sit and cleanse himself with a towel. So many layers of filth have deposited on his body! He finds no time to clean himself because of daily quick baths. As he has leisure today, he must rub himself clean. Dinesh smeared the soap and rubbed the dirt off his neck, hands, legs and back. Now, pleasant thoughts started creeping into his mind. Dinesh felt that his mind has also been cluttered with ugly thoughts. Once in a while, one must get rid of them by keeping the mind free. The mind also needs rest, to rear healthy thoughts. After the bath, Dinesh went straight to the hotel and returned home finishing his lunch there.

The day was very hot. He was very thirsty. As he opened the freeze for water, he recalled the foul smell. It would have been better, had he cleaned the freeze before his bath and switched it on. At least he could have got cold water to drink, he thought. Dinesh knew that there was no water in the pitcher either and the water of the steel drum was undrinkable. So, he decided to clean the freeze first.

Dinesh opened the freeze and pinched his nose due to the offensive smell. He drew the vegetable tray out and threw the rotten ones. He was left with a few eggplants, pointed gourds, tomato, a piece of ginger, and chilli pepper which he stored for future use. He threw the collected water of the tray in the bathroom, cleaned the bottles, stored a filled water bottle in the deep freeze chamber and switched on the freeze. By now, he was sweating profusely. Can he manage in such hot weather?

Dinesh, at once remembered the air cooler. As he switched it on, hot air blew out of it. The water had dried up. So he needed to fill it. The tanks in the bathroom too were dry. The maid servant had not come since two days. A bit of water was left in the pitcher. But, the motor of the cooler can hardly lift so less amount of water. Better to pour water by opening the upper lid of the cooler to wet the side pads. But a host of things have to be removed from the top of the cooler as it was serving like a table. After removing the brush stand, soap case, oil bottle, a few cups and saucers, two glasses, an aluminium pot and a few empty jars, he could open the upper lid to pour water of the steel drum into it. 'Will think of water later. First may life be saved from heat.' The air felt cool to his body. When he turned the blow of air towards the bed to take a nap, he found that the bed is cluttered with a host of things. He thought that, it may take him an hour to remove them. So he decided to lie down on the floor. But the floor was dirty as it had not been dusted for the last two days. Besides, the toys of Jiten were lying scattered. His own dress, *lungi*, towel, shorts, that he had left hastily two days earlier, were lying in a heap on the floor. Besides the spilled milk had dried up making it sticky. Luckily, because of the previous sleepless night, he had a sound sleep last night, or Dinesh fails to manage in such an unkempt place. He searched out a broom stick and by the time he cleaned the floor up, it was three o'clock in the afternoon.

Dinesh now rolled onto the bed. At once he remembered that he had purchased a pen. Whom should he write a letter? Recalling his friends, he was dozing off. Right at that time, he got up startled by a clangour. He saw the same naughty cat stood staring at him, its tail erect. It as if chided him, "You rascal mean fellow! Don't you keep anything to eat? Jiten's mom keeps the house filled with milk, curd, ghee and fish. It was in vain that I came here skipping seven other houses in this hot afternoon."

Suddenly Dinesh saw a pickle jar tilted and jaggary along with oil, spilling out of it. Probably its cap was loose. Close to it, the mustard container was toppled and the content scattered through out the room. Dinesh had purchased two kg of it because he got at a cheaper price. Now, two kg of mustard dispersed and drifting through out the room. Dinesh picked up a few grains and started counting. He can never count them in one whole life. He cannot collect them even if he toils for a full day. Using the broom, he may need a full day to gather them. If Ritu sees it, she will come to blows with him. So, he has to clean it first. She has gone since day before yesterday and may return by this evening being bored.

Dinesh switched off the fan and air cooler. The moving mustards stood still in their respective places. A few, of course, still tossed in a particular motion as if mocking at the leisure, Dinesh was enjoying. Dinesh swept them to a corner and while pouring them back to the container, he was thinking to call Ritu if she doesn't turn up today, "I am fed up, come soon, I am at leisure when you are at home, at least I get relief from the household chores." A handful of mustard was still left on the floor which Dinesh swept away and standing before the air cooler dried him. As he thought to lie down on the bed, he found oil and jaggary dripping from the tilted pickle bottle. Had Jiten been here now, he would have stood below it opening his mouth and swallowed away the dripping pickle. The dripping of pickle sauce seemed attractive to Dinesh. He stood up, fearing the whole floor to be sticky with it. First he thought to collect the drops in a glass. Then he brought a stool, stood upon it and straightened the pickle jar. As he thought to place the mustard container close to it, he detected a thick long trail of ants around the pickle jar.

How come so many ants did collect here? If the source is cleaned, the ants will go away by themselves, he thought. He traced their track and saw that, they emanated from the wall behind the mustard container in a straight line and bent up at the skylight to the other side. As he came to the other side, he traced them on the projection and below it, they trailed on the wall behind the dressing table, to the next wall and through a hole on the doorjamb, on to the outer veranda, down into the bathroom and to another wall and beyond. It was as if a river in spate, an endless army of ants. He couldn't understand why at all they were in his house if, there is nothing here. Are they using his house as a national highway? Dinesh, approaching nearer to the wall, marked their movement intently. Even if it appeared one single line, there were if fact two lines, as if an one way traffic. One line was moving eastward while the other westward. The westward movers were carrying some whitish food material in their mouth and the mouths of the eastward movers were empty. They seemed more in hurry and occasionally as if kissing other ants. Probably they were enquiring about the situation in the east from the returnees. Yet, whatever it is, their busyness on a war footing was as if, a rebuff to the summer heat. Dinesh pondered, can this flow be checked? Can their track be altered? It could be their emergency tracks not their usual one. Dinesh came up with a broomstick and contemplated, what do I gain by disturbing them when they don't hurt me? Still Dinesh, without reason, agitated them with the broom. For sometime, the ants ran helter-skelter, the flow seemed broken though, after sometime, the flow again streamlined. This time they appeared busier than before.

While observing the ants, somehow Dinesh was struck with another queer thesis. It was evening. As he put on his dress, with a plan to get out of home, the power went off. In the darkness of the house, he could not locate a matchbox. He could not locate a candle or a lantern. While searching, he felt that the dust tea container fell off the shelf. But he didn't worry. Nothing worried him, the exit of Ritu, her absence, or her non-arrival, nothing worried him. Silently, he came out onto the street. Today he had detected a bare truth of life. Dinesh, with a supreme satisfaction, absorbed in self, set out on a stroll across the town.

CHAPTER THIRTEEN

Sobhan's Address

Subhendu had been extremely bored that day. That day he realised for the first time, what blunder he committed by seeking a transfer to this township. Was he getting less bored in the previous town where he was placed earlier? Still he felt as if the boredom here is much more than that of his previous station. Yet, he failed to locate the exact cause of boredom, whenever he tried to find it out.

Everything was alright there. He had kept himself busy. He didn't have the leisure to even think of himself. Suddenly one day he got bored there. He felt as if, he is stuck somewhere in the midst of the current. And that day Subhendu decided that he must move out of this place. That was all. He didn't put a second thought to it. He didn't choose a place to move on and mentioned the same in the request letter for transfer that he would not object towards any place of posting. Thus he was transferred to this place.

Everyone was stunned with his transfer order. He too was no less astonished that day. Because, transfer order within a week was beyond his expectation also. Still, he was cool, neither sorry nor happy. Everyone forbade him to move out. But, he didn't pay a heed to anyone. What exactly had happened to him?

A few colleagues even forced him to wait for a few more days. But he didn't mind. Hence, that was Subhendu's last day in the office and the very next day, Subhendu left the office and the town so suddenly for the new place that no one could get a hint of his departure. It seemed as if, he had left the place on a long vacation. Subhendu, out of suffocation had come away and since then had not left this town. Today, after full two years Subhendu again felt that he is dead bored here. What a mistake did he not commit by taking transfer to this place!

Subhendu sensed more pain as soon as he realised that he is getting bore. Because, first of all he didn't know the cause of his boredom and secondly, he didn't have a panacea to recoup from it. He waited for the postman every day who delivered useless official letters only and letters to others but never one to him. Whenever the phone rang, he thought if someone is calling him but, the peon came to call else one, not him and he gets bored. Isn't there anyone to miss him?

Once he got bored, Subhendu missed his previous office. As and when he sipped a cup of tea, he missed Laxman's tea stall of the previous town, the make shift bench under the silk cotton tree, where he used to spend his entire time excluding the office hours and discussion on poetry and literature over tea. He used to wait for Sobhan, Nirakara and Suman babu and along with tea and cigarette, every sitting turned to an assembly of poetry recitation.

These days as he steps into the office, he feels as if locked in a vacuum chamber, as if a barrier erected between every two staff members. There is only work and work and work here. Nothing beyond work, no humour, no merrymaking, no discussion, no communication, no link amongst the staff members. Who is it that shut their mouths up? Subhendu doesn't like this way of things. Only five numbers of staffs are there but no harmony amongst them? Wasn't Subhendu happy there in his previous office? He used to get bored if he missed office for a single day. The office was as if a play ground for him. A day of leave from office seemed to him, a deprivation of one happy day of life. Truly he was very happy those days, in the previous office, in that township. Why at all did he take such a decision?

Subhendu missed all these so much that he lost the zeal to work. He wished to go back to the previous town in an instant, at least for a few days. No doubt Subhendu is missing all of them so much but would any one be missing him there too? Once upon a time, everything used to stand still there in absence of Subhendu. Everything awaited his opinion. How all those activities would be running these days? No place remains vacant in absence of any one probably, no one is inevitable for any job probably, time manages in its own way, reflected Subhendu.

While occupied in such shards of thoughts, Subhendu heard the telephone ringing and saw none picking it up. Subhendu went near the phone slowly and picked up the receiver, "Hello! Hello! State Bank!" Someone from the other side was shouting "Hello! Hello!" loudly, though a snapping voice was reaching this side. Now Subhendu asked loudly from this side, "Hello! Whom do you need? Who is it? Where from you are calling?" Subhendu realised that, it was a trunk call. It has to be an urgent call. So, even though he was not in mood, still he was unable to hang up, being under the spell of guilty conscience. Gradually the clarity of the voice from the other side improved, "Hello! Is Subhendu there? Can you please call him?"

"Yes, this is Subhendu speaking. Who is it?" Again the voice crackled. Subhendu got worried. Who could it be calling from such a distance, yet he failed to identify? Again Subhendu shouted into the phone, "Subhendu here! Who is it calling?"

"Oh, Subhendu! Is that you? Hello!" Asked the speaker from the other side.

"Come to Sambalpur tomorrow. You must have holiday tomorrow? Hello! This is Sobhan here. By six o'clock we will be at Sukanta Babu's place. Try, by six o'clock!" After that, despite several hellos, the voice died out. Subhendu placed the receiver back, went out to light a cigarette and remembered Sobhan.

After Subhendu came off that town, Sobhan also had left. He too had wished for, some what an exile. After he left that town, he did write a letter to Subhendu. Subhendu of course could not recall if he had answered him back then. But since then there was a loss of contact. And today, suddenly Sobhan had invited him to Sambalpur. Tomorrow and the day after were holidays. Is Sobhan once again getting bored there?

Subhendu, the same night it self prepared to set out for Sambalpur. He put his old diary, his new poetry, stories, a pen, toothbrush, toothpaste, *lungi*, shorts and towel in a bag. Pondering over many things like, what will he do at Sambalpur, where will he stay, whom will he meet, how Sambalpur will feel to him, how will the friends behave, will they be happy or wonder, will the tea stall of Laxman be there, what will be his remark on him and the like, he went to bed.

On reaching Sambalpur, Subhendu finds the nights immensely lengthy. The entire town is as if dead in sleep. Subhendu roams through out the town but tumbles upon no body. He knocks at every door but opens nobody. Subhendu, out of fatigue sleeps at the church veranda. Someone in the church appears like the church father, though gowned black. He approaches Subhendu carrying a crutch. His face is indistinct behind his beards. Waking up Subhendu he tells, "the night is endless here, neither the day breaks. That night while leaving this town, you took away the church bell. Since then, no more does it toll. The folks are fast asleep since that night. May the God pardon you, please return back the bell." The church father searches his bag and rescues a big bell.

Subhendu is scratching his head, if he has ever seen such a bell. It is designed like the face of a tiger. Two ferocious eyes on it and a tongue acting like the clapper of the bell. His bag didn't contain any thing such. Subhendu remembers to have placed an old diary, his new poetry, stories, a pen, toothbrush, toothpaste, lungi, shorts and towel which were missing from his bag. But in lieu, he finds a pistol, a knife, a few hand bombs, a book of bible and a pool of blood in the bag. Subhendu fearfully gazes at the pretender who is now riding a horse as a dacoit and says, "I am off with this bell. I don't care if the night ends or not. If ever the day breaks, you will be picked up as the killer. I have silenced the church father once for all. Subhendu finds that, the church father is lying injured with a bullet and bleeding in his chest. He runs at the Church father and shouts, 'Murder! Murder!' and breaks his slumber. It is morning. His pounding heart resembles the hammering of a '*dhenki*' (manual pounder) whose sound is audible from the nearby house. What a nightmare!

Subhendu washes his face, brushes his teeth and is served a cup of tea. As Subhendu prepares to leave for Sambalpur, the time of bus slips by. Subhendu decides to catch the afternoon bus. After lunch, he takes a nap and thinks, "Bus journey is too boring. They pause at every stop." Subhendu, since long has not travelled in a bus. So, he decides to ride the bike to Sambalpur. The speedometer shows forty, fifty, sixty, as if a pair of wings have cropped up on his flanks after a long time. He rams on the throttle. He curses the trucks, "Rascals, they don't leave a bit of space to any one else." His elbows ache. He stops and lights a smoke. He stops over the Mahanadi Bridge and takes a view of the Hirakud dam overwhelmingly.

Sambalpur is approaching and the time is only one quarter left to six. He has to reach Sambalpur by Six anyhow, not to upset the plans. Subhendu is spent, his elbow is aching. He is stretching on the bike, still trying to reach on time. Crossing the *Ainṭhāpalichowk*, he nears the LIC office building. The traffic is choked. The gate at the level crossing is down. It's time for the express train to pass. What an ill-luck! Subhendu snails through the congested traffic, his bike on first gear, blowing the horn and now he is obstructed by a mini bus. A rickshaw comes in from a side. A few men come from the front. Everyone is jostling to escape the crowd. The vegetables of a seller scatter on the road. A street dog is scurrying, as if it also has to board the train.

Subhendu turns to the *Gopālmal* lane. He pauses before the house of Sukanta. His for year old daughter Pinki comes out carrying a toy. Subhendu asks her, *"Pinki! Bābā kothāye?"* (Where is your dad, Pinki!)

"Off to market."

"Why?"

"To get chalk for me."

Boudi, Sukanta's wife comes out. She speaks a Bengali mixed broken Odia, "Just now Sukanta left for the market with Nirakara and Sobhan. It's less than ten minutes. They were expecting you. Even waited for long."

Subhendu looks at his watch. Its ten minutes past six. He is late by ten minutes. He feels annoyed, "Since when these folks became so punctual?" He thought, as the train has not yet left, they mustn't have gone too far in the crowd.

Subhendu starts his bike and returns back, wondering if they would be waiting for him at the railway station. The train is passing. Subhendu is intently looking between the gap of every two compartments, if he can locate one of them. Someone from the nearby scooter greets him. Though the man appears known, he fails to recall him. Even if he smiles at the person, he fails to pay due attention to him. Trucks and buses honk behind him. The last boggy of the train crosses. The same scene on the other side of the gate, as if one apple has been split open into two equal parts. Up goes the gate. Even if Subhendu feels that his head might hit the gate, he sneaks beneath it.

He locks the bike at Khan Pan Shop and looks around. A few bonny girls come out of the station but, he has no time, despite his wishes to ogle at them. He looks into the tea stall, but finds none. Then he enters the platform, looks at the farthest end, searching for three loitering men in the crowd. Three men, one of them tall, two short. One fair two others dark. One bald, rest two with hair. One wears a pair of specs the other two without them. But, all the three carry beard on cheek and chin. Where are three such men lost whom Subhendu is unable to find? The trio have to be at some tea stall or pan stall, or lost in discussion on some new poetry in front of some news stall. Subhendu has to locate three such me, who would be ambling over gossips. They mustn't be having a fixed destination; still they would be just moving.

Subhendu, approaching the news stand at *Phāṭak* asks for Sobhan. The stall owner answers, "Yes, they were here. They left just now. But, where to, I have no idea." Subhendu combs the rest of the pan and tea stalls nearby but fails to find them. He goes to all those probable spots where in the past they used to spend hours together reciting poetry and killing time.

He heads for Laxman's tea stall. Laxman is elated to find him. He says, "Just now all your three friends were here. They too were asking for you, as you are doing now." Laxman serves him tea. Subhendu denies, but takes it. Laxman asks him about his wellbeing, about his long absence, about his non arrival in the mean time and how his stall has been empty since Subhendu left. Subhendu listens to him and sips tea.

Now he turns his bike towards the bus stand. There, at the Bishnu book stall, Bishnu too repeats the same story, "Just a moment back all the three were here." Subhendu searches for them at every nook and corner of the bus stand. But, there were as if untraceable. A number of familiar folks tumble upon him,

"Oh! Subhendu, is it you? How are you? Where were you for so long? Haven't you put on a bit flesh? But you look nice, handsome."

Avoiding everyone, Subhendu comes away. It's essential for him to search out Sobhan. He has lost interest in everything else. He lights a cigarette and dragging hard on it broods over again,

"Where should he head next? Should he head again to the *Phāṭak* railway station, or *Gol bazaar*, or *Gopalmal*, or *Baḍ bazaar*? Where could they go? Where could three full grown men disappear? Standing at the traffic chowk, Subhendu is lost in thoughts. The traffic man runs at him, "Why did you stop in the middle of the crossing? Move on. Vacate the road."

Subhendu locks his bike at Punjab hotel. He walks down up to*Gol bazaar* and returns. Again he heads up to the *Phāṭak* railway station and comes back.

Now Subhendu takes to the Ashoka talkies road. It was interval break of the evening show. He meets a number of his acquaintances. He sips tea with them, puffs smoke and heads up to the Jail chowk and returns back. Again he recalls his friends, shouldn't he haveproceededahead?

He finds three men coming from a distance. One of them resembles Sobhan. The taller one is walking just like Sukanta babu. Subhendu is relaxed, at last.... He plans out how to greet them on arrival. He brings back his bike and rides in that direction but, the trio as if vanish into thin air. Subhendu asks the man at the nearby pan stall, "Where are the barbate trio, who were here just now?" The man points at Amarji hotel. Subhendu is bewildered, least convinced, yet enters the hotel to find three men toasting three jugs of beer. No, he was not searching for them. They were different. Subhendu returns. The Punjabi owner asks him in Hindi, "What would you like to have Sir! Please be seated. Why are you in so hurry?" Answering him "Later" Subhendu comes out.

A beggar approaches him speaking Hindi, "Eaten not a grain since two days *Babuji*! Give me something to eat! May God bless you *Babuji*!" His withered belly has sunk into his back. He is carrying a stick and a tin can and his eyes, as if accumulated an endless search for someone since centuries. Greying hair, unkempt beard, dirty ragged *dhoti*. Subhendu fishes out a fifty paisa coin to give him. A few drunk are shouting at each other. A man is lying senseless under the light post. A lad is tightening nut bolt in a nearby garage, sweat dripping off his head and muscles of his arm swelling. Subhendu, in his mind is asking to all of them, "Did you see Sobhan? Sobhan! Sobhan was one of those trio, who left home at six in the evening, a bit bald on head, carries a bunch of beard on his chin, dark complexioned, but his eyes, brighter than the rest two. That is Sobhan. I am asking for him. Did you meet him?"

Subhendu is now walking the *Dhankauḍā road*. He stops at the place of Shabbir babu. Shabbir babu is pleased to find him. It was after a long time that, Subhendu is meeting him. "Subhendu! What are your writings these days?" Shabbir babu is narrating his sorrows, his ailing wife, his child who burnt in fire, his frail financial condition, his loss of job, the tumult over some of his writings, non payment of royalty by the publishers, form fill up expenses of his children, medicines, saree for his wife, dress for his eldest daughter, lingering credit at the provision stores, inadequacy of rice and scarcity of vegetables at home. Subhendu sits dumb, listens to everything. A lot has changed within the last two years. He feels his throat drying up. Asking for a glass of water he gurgles down his throat.

Then he asks about Sobhan. Shabbir babu answers, "He had come, but left just now. He was talking of translation of some poems." Subhendu gets up to leave. Shabbir Bhāi asks him to sit a bit more. But Subhendu kick starts his bike and takes one more round of the town. Next what, he ponders. He goes to Ashoka talkies. No. He cannot catch Sobhan any more. He buys a ticket and enters the cinema hall.

A hero comes up on the screen. A heroine and a bearded villain too appear. A song floats on. The plot of this film seems same to Subhendu. He can guess what will come up in the next scene and gets bored. It's all similar. There is nothing new in the story. He comes out of the hall opening the gate. The guard is asleep. He brawls with him and brings out his bike.

While starting the bike he thinks, now what to do? He takes the road towards GM College. He locks the bike at the mess near the book stall. It is mid-night. The friends in the mess must be asleep. He didn't like to disturb them and heads for the GM college ground. He opens up the button of his shirt. He wipes his face with the handkerchief. So many times he has enjoyed here poetry recitation with Sobhan. Subhendu rolls on the ground. It is a moonlit summer night. A pleasant breeze is blowing. The zephyr is as if bringing him back the poems recited by Sobhan. Whatever Subhendu is seeing are as if images of Sobhan's poems. His eyes are shutting down. Until morning, he falls asleep there.

As he gets up in the morning, he decides not to search for Sobhan anymore. He has touched many people, relations, acquaintances, near and dear, kith and kin, friends, poets and intellectuals. No more he will search for Sobhan. He has acquired the true address of Sobhan, reflects Subhendu.

Next morning, he heads for the home of Sukanta babu. *Boudi* comes out wiping her hands in one end of her saree. Trailing her comes Pinki, carrying a pen in her hand.

She speaks her usual Bengali mixed broken Odia, "Dad is not home. Don't know where he went."

Boudi says, "They searched for you a lot yesterday. But, could not meet. Sobhan left by the night train. Nirakara left by the morning train. Sukanta babu has gone to some lodge to attend some of his friends from Rourkela."

Subhendu starts his bike. No, he won't search for Sobhan. He needs not search any more. He remembers the wild dream of last night. In one go, for seventy kilometres, he rides back to his village. His sister comes out and asks,

"How come you are back? Had you not been off for two days?"

Subhendu removes his shoes and socks, changes from trousers and shirt to a *lungi*. He washes his face. Sips the tea and lies down on the bed. He recalls an incident of last night. Yes. He did meet Sobhan. He met him everywhere - at the crowd of the shut level crossing, at every tea and pan stall, at the cinema hall, at the toasting of the three bearded drinkers, in the hunger struck eyes of the beggar, in the dripping sweat of that garage boy, in all the sorrows of Shabbir babu, at the bus stand, at the railway platform, at the ground of GM College, in that senseless drunkard lying under the light post and all these are his real address. Subhendu hazily remembers his madly search of the previous evening. Subhendu speaks to himself,

"I did meet you Sobhan. I met you at every lane and every crossroad, in my mind and my heart, and in every bit of my silence, I met you."

CHAPTER FOURTEEN

Dream city

Sambit, on return from class, unlaces the shoes from his fatigued feet and lying on the bedfagged, gazes at the sky through the open window. He gazes at the stretching mountain range, feelingworn out, leaning against the window. Why does he feel lonely despite having so many friends?

He sits bending over the table and gazes at the table top. The table is adjacent to the bed. A row of various books arranged against the wall. A stake of magazines placed at one corner of the table, varieties of pens in a pen stand, two to three empty cigarette cartons, a dirty ash tray, a bunch of bits of papers and two to three number of open books.

Sambit stretched himself. Looked into his face on the mirror. Straightened his unkempt hair a bit. Unbuttoned his shirt. Struck a match and threw at the floor. Then threw his shirt onto the rack. Tidied the table a bit. Whistled a Hindi film song. Lighted an incense stick and pondered to recite a poem. From the row of books, he dragged out the "Anthology of modern poetry" edited by John Wain and flipped through the pages -

"Love! Love! A Lily is my care
She is sweeter than a tree
Loving I use the air
Most lovingly I breathe."

Neither song nor poetry, nothing appeals him. What Sambit will do now? Quietly, placing his head on the table top he thought to dwell upon something.

Abinash, his room mate has been chattering for sometime but Sambit as if turned deaf. Stupid fellow. Let him carry on. How long one can sit silently? A host of unwanted thoughts creepinto his mind. Sambit considers hollering out to shatter the silence. What Sambit should do now? Go to sleep? No, he cannot. Go out side? But he came in just now. Spar at Abinash? No need. Then what to do?

Sambit is sitting quiet. A chunk of the busy campus is visible through the opening of the widow. Beyond it stretch vast expanse of meadows and then the zigzag mountain range. A load of darkness has entered the room though it is just evening outside. Whether he should study, switching on the light or idle, in the darkness. Abinash is flat on his bed. Let the lazy scamp sleep. Sambit switched on the light and hitting a fisticuff on his back said, "Sleep off O scamp sleep! And die in your sleep!"

"So what, if I sleep or not, so what if I die or not! Why don't you sleep? You just keep staring blank, stupid! Nothing comes true by thinking only. You have to act for what you wish." Abinash fell back to sleep dragging a sheet over his face. After a few moments, his snoring echoed in the whole room.

Idiot! Stupid! Silly fool! Sambit, tore an empty carton of cigarette into pieces, threw them at Abinash, put on his shirt and went out of the room banging the door behind him.

Sambit, while sipping tea at Rama canteen felt that all the boys are prattling. So after tea, he lighted a cigarette and headed on the guest house road. Finding the tiny temple beside the road he entered. Mocking at the *"Siva Linga"* (Phallic Symbol) he said, "You are the only lucky one, Bro! Enjoying happily. Bravo! Bravo!" Then for sometime, he watched the children playing at the courtyard of the temple and deplored that needlessly he was growing up.

Sambit, on his way back to the hostel, paused before the ladies' hostel, expecting to have a glance of a pretty face or two through some open window and felt like shouting at them, "O dear girls! Jump out of your windows and enjoy the enchanting moonlit night outside." But, uttering not a single word, he withdrew to his hostel.

Abinash is still asleep. Let the poor lazy remain asleep.

Sambit, bringing out the book "In memoriam", pondered over Mita. But, recalling the reproach of Prof. Nayak, he decided to discard Mita from his mind. He is scoldedevery time by the professor yet fails to recall a single line of this book. The professor questions him on it and he remains silent. Why doesn't he read it - whether he doesn't like "In Memoriam", or because it's a long poem, or any other reason? Perhaps, these days he thinks more of Mita; the more he thinks, the lonelier he feels.

What is his relation with Mita?

Abinash turned his side. Coughed. Itched his neck. Slapped his back thinking of a mosquito. Abinash, the poor lazy fellow, let him be asleep.

Sambit changed to a *lungi*. Went to the bathroom for a wash. Dried himself with a towel. Humming a song, tried to wake up Abinash, "You shit! Get up. It's class time."

Abinash got up startled and reached for his toothbrush. Sambit mocked, "Stupid! Can't you guess whether it's day or night? It's ten o'clock. Let's go for dinner."

On the mess table, there was an endless discussion on various poets. While washing hands, Abinash said, "What I see, without poetry, you fail to digest your food these days."

Ajay said, "Food can be digested but you need digestive pills for pebbles."

Abinash rolled onto the bed with a magazine and said, "Switch off the light and go to sleep."

"Don't you have any other job?Just eat, sleep and die... Savage fellow!"

"The second semester if far away. It may postpone even. What will you get by rote learning since now? See, I don't aim to top the batch. If you hanker for the gold medal, you are free to chase. I am off to sleep."

Sambit sat down with the "In memoriam" and decided to memorise it, digest it and face any question of any professor the next day. He flipped through the book.

"Why didn't you come to class yesterday?"

"How does it matter to you, if I am present or absent?"

"It does matter, hence I asked."

"How?"

"Stupid"

"Be straight"

"Everything is not said straight. Or, how will it make a poetry."

"Now, is it a poetry?"

"Life itself is a long poetry and every event, a line of it."

"I am allergic to lengthy poems and hence, 'In memoriam' is not my cup of tea."

The magazine ruffled over the face of Abinash. Sambit came to senses. He rebuked himself vehemently, "Rascal, lewd, you stray only hither and thither. Repeatedly I urged upon you to read the poem, but you think only of Mita." Sambit picked up the Filmfare magazine from the face of Abinash and addressing Rekha's picture as if to Mita's, adjured,"Please Mita, allow me to read." Then he placed the magazine on the table and wished good night to the light bulb, switched it off and jumped over to the bed. He looked, once at the ladies' hostel, the dark mountain, the empty road, the row of lights of Hirakud Dam. He dragged the sheet over Abinash, sang a lullaby to him patting on his back and still thinking of Mita, went to sleep.

Sambit, as woke up in the morning, searched for Abinash beside him. But he had vanished. He sat up and looked through the window. The sun had risen high up. Boys and girls in group were headed for the class. He supposed it must be nine o'clock. And Prof. Nayak's class was at nine. Get late, and "In memoriam" will upbraid, he thought. He searched for the toothbrush. The toothpaste tube was empty. Only a bit can be squeezed out by excessive force. What is this daily affair of brushing the teeth, combing the hair? He didn't have time to look at the mirror. So, he fished out the general note book while combing his hair by his fingers. He didn't find a pen. So, he headed for the class with the note book and a library book.

The class had commenced. Sambit, silently stood at the door.

"Sambit! Again you are late?"

"Sorry Sir!" Said Sambit.

"Come in. So, in the last class, I was telling about..." Prof. Nayak continued with the lecture.

Sambit went to the last bench and opened up his general note book. He asked Bhaben for a pen. In a hushed up voice he said, " I got only one. Don't worry, we will share it."

Sambit closed his general note book down. No need to write any thing. He can remember everything just by listening.

The professor carried on with his lecture. Sambit tried to listen to him.

Mita today has come clad in a saree. It seems she wrapped it first time today and that is why, she is dragging the end repeatedly. She seems uneasy with it. But, it suits her fine. He waited for the class to finish and thought to tell her. Should he only tell her or recite Akshyaya Mohanty's, *"Sāḍhi pindhi helu bhāri siyāṇī"* (Seem you matured in a saree). But, Mita may be offended with the song. Besides will he dare sing before her? Let him first speak about her wearing the saree. Hah! What's the harm in appreciating a beauty?

Mita is turning back. Is she looking for Sambit or searching for one else? Everyone had started looking back, one by one, at him. What's the matter, Bhaben shook him, "Hey you! Sir is asking you something." Sambit shuddered from tip to toe. He stood up. Everyone jeered at him. Sir was asking, "Do you know it?" Sambit kicked Bhaben, "What did Sir ask?"

"Did you hear the question? I think you are unmindful," growled Prof. Nayak.

"Yes Sir!"

"If you are neither attentive, nor have interest in my class, why do you come at all? I will give you attendance. Please get out of my class."

Sambit felt truly hurt. He went out of the class, wiping sweat with his handkerchief and abused Mita in his mind, "Why did you come wearing a saree today? You come out of the class and I will see you."

Sambit was miffed standing at the corridor and remembered that he didn't have tea since morning. So he went to Rao canteen and sat down there placing an order for a hot single tea. Lighting a cigarette he blew the smoke up into the air.

Prof. Panda was on leave. So the classes ended by twelve o'clock. Discussing about the picnic spot as they walked on, Sambit told Mita, "Let's go to the library?"

Sambit, while combing through the Odia bookshelves said, "Here is a good poetry book, 'Saptama Ritu' (The seventh season). Would you like to read it?"

"I don't like Odia poetry."

"Seems you puffing up with conceit as a student of English?"

"I just don't like, nothing else" said Mita.

Sambit was expecting Mita to ask him why he was inattentive in the class. But she didn't. So he too couldn't pass onto her that the saree suited her very much. And that, he was mulling over that. Or, could he have told her in some different way? Mita was heading towards the English bookshelves to find out a book on literary criticism.

Sambit casually called Mita back.

"What is it?" Mita asked.

"Why did you come today wearing a saree?"

Mita blushed a bit. She probably expected Sambit to tell next that it suited her well.

"So what? It was just a wish."

"Why didn't you wish it earlier?"

"How does it trouble you?"

"I said, because it troubles me. All the troubles are not revealed. Could everything be conveyed, there wouldn't be anything called trouble. Do you know, life itself is a mega trouble. Every event is but one more step leading to another trouble."

Mita smiled, "I don't appreciate troubles. Ok. Henceforth I will not drape in a saree and cutting a side glance at Sambit, meaningfully said "Bye...""

Sambit got the book *"Saptama Ritu"* issued in his name and left for the hostel. Abinash was readying for a nap after lunch. Sambit put his note book on the table and flipped on the news paper.

"Hey! Again a war between Iran and Iraq."

"Did you finish lunch?"

"Yet to brush my teeth."

"Rascal crazy man! It's one o'clock afternoon. When will you bathe?"

"Will this war ever end?" Sambit came up with the toothbrush.

"First go and eat your lunch. Then brush and bathe, or the mess will close."

"That's the fate of oil-money, you know. Purchase weapons and fight. America, to sell weapons, has engaged everyone in war. You will see, when you get up tomorrow morning, you will find India will be at war and I, holding a machine gun, would be fighting at the borders. And you lazy lousy, would be slumbering here. If ever a bomb drops, may it explode on your chest."

"O yes! The Govt. is just searching for rickety men like you to induct as commanders of army. Dirty lunatic! You didn't bathe since fifteen days, didn't brush teeth since two days, didn't comb hair since twenty days and God knows, what you ate and when. You don't care to study, only worry about girls in the classroom even. You will die, you will fail. Let me sleep."

After lunch, Sambit opened Eliot. "Speak! Speak! Why do you never speak! Speak!"

Sambit memorised the line and decided to speak it to Mita next day. If Mita felt hurt, he can easily twist that he was quoting Eliot and intended her to explain the meaning.

Sambit, supporting the pillow against the wall, reclined on it. Puffing the smoke he reflected, "Life is a real trouble." Bravo! a great philosophy has escaped his lips. Mita will brood over him a lot today. Let her miss him and die.

Mita, why don't you die? I could write an "In memoriam" for you. Sambit held a long moot on whether he will be aggrieved by the death of Mita. But, failing to reach a conclusion, he decided to write down a poem at least musing Mita to be dead. Sambit, calculated in this regard that, whatever poem he would write at the death of Mita, will measure not less than ten to fifteen pages long. Hardly any reader will feel inclined to read it and by means of push and pull, if it is included in some syllabus, the students will resent a lot. Thus, he decided not to take up such a temerarious job. After all, Mita is not yet dead. We would see when she is dead.

As the glow of the cigarette singed his finger, he learnt that, he has been wasting time behind useless thoughts. He has not told Mita any thing. Only his one-sidedobsession for her has possessed him like some spook. Of course, he is confident that Mita does love him. Yet, there has not been any formal deed of agreement or consent between them. Still, in what manner such a firm truth should be proposed at Mita? Is it essential to speak out 'I love you'? Even if it is expressed, how to do it?

Sambit planned out two to three styles. But not a single appealed him. So he dragged out from the bookshelf, the complete works of Shakespeare. A rat jumped out of the bookshelf, landed on the back of Abinash and escaped through the window. Startled Abinash stared at Sambit angrily and shouted, "Why do you scratch me? If you don't feel sleepy, get lost into that journal section to read." And Abinash relapsed to his slept, dragging the sheet over him.

Sambit, was not impressed by the ideas, what he deduced from Shakespeare. They were old fashioned. So he resolved to write a research based book on "How to dote on a girl" and headed for the journal section, to gather the required material on the chosen topic.

Sambit, there in the journal section, found Prof. Nayak pouncing upon a blackish book. He thought that Sir might look down upon him, if he finds him reading some cheap book. So he took up a "Times" magazine and started reading Iraq-Iran war. Three times raising his eyes he peeked at Prof. Nayak. But, Prof. Nayak was glued to the book, perhaps he was memorising it in toto. Even if Prof. Nayak drove Sambit many times out of his class, Sambit still reared a lot of respect for him.

Sambit was now reading on F-16. Prof. Nayak came up to him and asked, "Interested in world affairs?"

"Yes Sir, preparing for civil services." Sambit said.

"Very good. Carry on." He then pushed the fat book towards Sambit and said, "A nice book, 'Sociology of Literature'. Read it, may be of great help."

Sambit, not only read what he was reading, but started noting down. As he raised his head, Prof. Nayak was not there. He looked around and was assured that Sir had left. Or, he had planned to clear his doubts on a few topics. Again he thought that, it was good. He will put forth his doubts tomorrow in the classroom and startle all, including Mita. At least, let everyone be free of the misconception that, Sambit is not studious.

Sambit checked time from the watch of the fellow sitting next to him. It was five o'clock, time to head for Rama canteen. So, putting the book back at the right place, he set out.

At the Rama canteen, a few students of Political Science, English and Economics were debating on the political situation of Odisha over *muḍhi* (puffed rice) and mixture. Sambit ordered for a tea and ate a fistful of *muḍhi* from a plate. In lieu of that handful of *muḍhi* they demanded for Sambit's opinion on an intricate political matter of Odisha. But, he didn't have interest in such a question. So, Sambit replied, "I know not a thing on matters of Odisha or India, not even interested much."

They were neither happy with his reply nor prepared to spare him so easily. Ajay intervened, "So you, as if know the whole world, save Odisha!" Sambit felt offended with the banter.

Sambit had got his tea. He ordered, "Will you send a fag Rama!"and turned to Ajay, "Of course, may not be so minutely, yet enough to serve my need." Ajay was a dullard in world affairs even though he refers to "The Samāja" at times. So, Sunil of Political Science quizzed him. Sambit, along with satisfactory answers to all the questions, delivered a short speech on world affairs. His knowledge was simply unbelievable on the part of everyone. They were so elated that, they applauded shouting, "Bravo! Bravo! Very soon you are sure to crack the civil services. Only you need to have an eye on situation of India." Boys of the other departments commented, "English boys come with some amount of grey cells." It was for the sake of Sambit that, the prestige of the department rose high and Ajay was not only happy but missed not the chance to take pride on behalf of Sambit. But, as Sambit was averse to such praises, he bade everyone good bye and took to the guest house road.

Sambit got into the tiny temple and addressed the Phallic Symbol, "You are the only lucky one, Bro! Enjoying happily." Then for sometime, he watched the children playing at the courtyard and deplored that needlessly he was growing up. While returning, he paused in front of the ladies' hostel and thought to call Mita. But decided otherwise as he himself was not sure how she would react. He tried to detect one or two pretty faces through the window and in his mind said, "O dear girls! Jump out of your windows and enjoy the enchanting moonlit night outside." He however withdrew to his hostel.

Abinash had not got up yet. Sambit switched on the light. Patting on the back of Abinash, he woke him up and said, "Won't you go to class?" As Abinash reached for his toothbrush and toothpaste, Sambit mocked at him, "Cannot you distinguish between day and night, you shit, cadaver? You are dead, when you are asleep. Why do you die when you are still alive? Open your eyes. Look at the world. There is a severe war between Iran and Iraq.The US Govt. is supplying all the weapons and war materials. Even there has been two attempts on India on it's border with Pakistan. As you get up tomorrow morning, you may find a bomb on your chest."

Abinash was still dozing off. But the way Sambit had uttered "Bomb", awoke Abinash fully. Hastily he came back washing his face and asked Sambit, "Where did the bomb drop?"

"Not yet dropped. But, will drop soon."

"Where?"

"On your face! Stupid fool. Why do you scare about bomb so much? Are you so fearful of your life?"

"No, no. Why should I be scared? But, one should stay informed about bomb *'fomb'*. Suppose someone asks somewhere, unless I have right information, shall I not make a fool of myself?"

Sambit laughed to his heart's content and caressing his hair said, "My dear, poor fellow! Be not so senseless in sleep! Go. Get some cool air and hot tea outside. We will start study."

Abinash put on his dress and went out.

Sambit opened up the Filmfare magazine and addressed to the picture of Rekha, "Alas Mita! How come since long, I didn't focus on you?" And he was lost in the imaginary dream land where he and Mita or Mita and he only exist.

CHAPTER FIFTEEN

A cockroach too has a heart

I was unaware that such a deadly snare had been spread for me.

My mind, that day was very much upset. So I thought, taking some outside air might relieve me. It was very hot inside. With one jump, I reached up to the corner of the door. Through the gap of the door and the doorjamb, I peeped outside. A few boys, drinking countless glassful, were creating a ruckus. So, I dared not go outside. If, someone chased me to kill, or crushed me under feet, or picked me up in hand for jesting, or clipped my pare of wings? No, I should not go outside. This building is Eden for me.

Just one lad stays here, who is present at times and absent at others. For a short while only, he stays here. A very calm and quiet boy. Still, with in the last two years, I couldn't understand him properly. He, placing his head on the pillow, looking through the window, always carries on brooding over something. Once in a while, he sits reading some book throughout the night. At times he writes pages after pages. Never does he keep his table neat and tidy. It remains always cluttered, everything remains scattered, the lad doesn't have a bit of leisure, he cleans the sooty spider webs never. At times he gazes at me in such a way that, being embarrassed I fail to look at him. I too have developed an attachment for him. Since a day or two, where did he go away that as if forgot to return back? He didn't even switch off the light, the fan is moving as it is and the window is stark open. The previous night of the day he left, he was seemingly disturbed. A bunch of papers he tore and threw away. He was smoking non stop, one after the other. Here on the floor lie those dirty ash and stubs of cigarettes. He was plucking his own hair whole night and throwing away the books on the table. Even he threw his shoes at one corner. I, out of fear to be hit by it, had receded to my home. But no, the lad is not like that. I know, I am in safe hands, as long as I stay with him. No one can kill me. Of late, I have developed an attachment for him. I do miss him if I don't see him for a day. When he stretches on his bed being tired, I feel inclined to caress his head a bit. I straight fly and land on his head. Does he feel tickled or what, he flicks his arm in an instant. I retreat. Don't know where he went away for so many days!

A continuous clang is audible from the kitchen. The sweet smell of cooking salivate me. I wish to have a round of the kitchen. But, it is very hot there. And to go there, I have to cut across other boys. So I restrained myself and jumped on to the table. There, I poking my antennae over crumbs of biscuits and mixture, dried up lime, onion peels, used tea glass and medicine wrappers, entered the books scattered and staked over the table. The soft pages of the books tickled my body. I, thinking to play hide and seek alone with myself in the cave of books, jumped over to the bookshelf where books were arranged. Till then, the lad sharing the room with me had not turned up. Above the book, the bright light was very hot. So, I jumped back to a dark corner of the room.

I had no idea that such a strong snare would be awaiting me there. I struggled, yet could not escape. The spider, waving her hands and legs gripped the gossamer web more tightly. My wings and legs were totally stuck. My whole body felt sticky. I swung a lot, tried to hop and jump. The more I tried to escape the more the tenuous fibre tangled me.

Occasionally while roaming about happily or dolefully, many times I have tumbled upon such spider webs. But, as they were intended for mosquitos, flies and other smaller insects, every time I have escaped by ripping the nets easily. But as it was not possible to tear this one apart, I wondered if the spider spun it so strong solely for me.

In spite of vigorous scrambling, I failed to get away. Now helplessly I looked at the spider. The look of the spider was calm, and amused; as if her eyes were telling me "You were fluttering a lot." I felt as if she was smiling over a cruel victory. I felt extremely limp. This was for the first time I was being overcome by somebody.

Probably she had not spread this net to devour me. I was actually much larger in size then she was. She can neither eat me alive nor kill me easily. For this, she has to wait for a week or so until I starve to death. She, neither can eat my wings nor my legs, nor can remove them from my body, nor can eat with them still on me. Surely, she mustn't have planned out such spic and span provisions for such a painful feasting, I thought. Thus, the spider's net was a mystery beyond my scope to decrypt.

The spider, with her popping eyes kept on staring at my helplessness. The way she contracted her legs that the whole web vigorously rocked, making me conscious of my helpless state. The spider once rushed towards me as if for a test and realising me totally in her grip, sat relaxed close by.

I told her, "Why do you harass me unnecessarily. Relieve me of this bondage. It has been extremely painful for me.

The spider said, "I only can entwine, I cannot untwine. I spread the web, yet don't lure anyone. Everyone falls into it by oneself. Gets vexed. But, I free everyone at a time, from two bondages.

The words of the spider chilled me. Do I have to die here this way or what; at once a craze for life sprouted in me. Just now, I remembered that lad, who was sharing with me my room. Had he been there he could hardly have tolerated my peril. I also realised that the spider is right, letting me loose is beyond her power. I cherished my past and helplessly I lay quiet there observing the spider's activities.

The spider, by now had gone away to one corner of her web. It was perhaps her kitchen. A load of food materials resembling *Tanduri chicken* were neatly stored there. She was humming some song while preparing her dinner. Outside from the mess, the clangouring of utensils was floating in air. The boys were busy in dinner in the noisy mess. Sweet smell of some dish emanated from the adjacent house. I felt hungry. I whispered soothingly at the spider, "I am ravenous. Please fix a bit for me as well. You don't plan to eat your dinner all alone, eh!"

"Fixing my dear, doing the same. You are my guest, shall I keep you famished? But you know, I am so poor, I can serve only what I eat. We will share what I have." My hunger, in a wink died out. Since long of course, no one had uttered such passionate words at me.

After dinner we sat together and gossiped a lot. The spider told me a host of stories of far and near and narrated a vast account of her solitary life. Besides, she narrated all her thoughts since the day she saw me here in this room, how I was tearing away all her cobwebs and she couldn't tell me anything despite her anger. She didn't forget to reveal the amount of affection she reared for me. But she kept on repeating the same questions to me, "Why do you live alone? Why do you like to stay alone? Lonely men, you know, are very cruel. You are cruel. You are a cockroach. Cockroaches are cruel. They don't have heart."

I was dead tired. As soon as I had my food, I felt sleepy. Even, I had dozed off once or twice, while being mindful of the chit-chat of the spider. I was of course heedless to her activities. But, the spider was very cunning. She instantly caught me dozing off. She, caressing my head and said tenderly, "Ah! So needlessly I have racked you for the whole day! You must have been tired of your struggle. Come, let me press your head a bit, you may feel relaxed." Before I knew, she pressed me from tip to toe. It was truly pleasing. What magic theses girls have in their hands? It was out and out awkward for me. After all, a girl she is and we two are all alone on one bed at such late hours of night? Along with a thrill I felt my body shudder. That very moment, the power failed. A holler of the lads from the nearby room started.

The spider by now had closed in to me and the way she was fondling my limbs that I had started perspiring. A quirky feeling was engulfing me. At once I asked her to go away, take rest, that it's already late and that I have been relieved of my fatigue. But did the spider pay any heed? She nestled into me and said, "Don't you sleep every night? Let's chat tonight." Implanting a sticky kiss on my lips she said, "So handsome you are, so stupid you are, still so heartless you are!" The spider now embraced me and jesting with me she said, "I love you." I was bewildered, even though by the flow of her hot breath, my ice cold heart was melting down. I was forced to play and wrestle with her for the entire night. By early morning, she was tired and the lids were drooping over her eyes due to an ultimate pleasure.

I told her, "Don't ever tangle me in the net of such illusion. It's very difficult to escape such labyrinth."

The spider that day, endlessly talked about love and entreated me, "You are so dear to me. Be not so heartless. Just stay entwined with me lifelong. You will learn how pleasant bondage is also. I will shower loads of love on you. We will lead a happy life together." The spider spoke a lot, giggled a lot, whined a lot, madly muttered a lot. Sobbing profusely she took refuge in my bosom. Fearing that I might go away, she clung to me so tight that, I remained imprisoned in her embrace until morning.

My head had grown very heavy by morning. She was neither able to meet my eyes out of abashment nor I could meet her eyes too. The very next moment, both of us grew emotional. Day long she questioned me on trivial matters, answering which was not easy. Considering her state of mind, I was not in a mood to make requests for my release. That day she attended to me a lot. Delicate dishes she served me to eat. Seating nearby she urged upon me to eat the sumptuous meal. She spread me a soft web to sleep and pressed my legs unhesitatingly. She seemed to have transformed to a devoted wife in just one night. Ah, The poor lass! I was grieving for her.

Amidst delight and grief, love and tear of the spider, passed on time so fast that, I too gradually forgot the bondage and stopped struggling in her web. When the spider was busy, I kept on brooding over her, grieving for her and repeating this question to self that, do cockroaches really have hearts, have hearts, have hearts, have love, have love, have love, have life, have life, have life?

Around this time, the lad sharing my room alone with me turned up. This time he appeared very happy. He was whistling a song, his stepping resembled dancing, as if he had found out something what he had been seeking for a long time.

He made the bed. Dusted the books and shelves. Tidied the table. Cleared the soot with a broomstick. Whistling a song, clearing the spider webs he now approaches the corner. He looks at the web. He looks at me struggling in it. Now he ponders over something. Again he looks at me struggling. He, picking me out of the web, cleans my wings and frees me into the air, "Go away, you too take to your wings happily." Happily, I zoom outside.

I remember the spider. I don't see her any more. Now every nook and corner is clean by the broomstick of the lad. The spider may also have escaped somewhere.

The lad now takes bath after the cleaning session. He, lighting an incense stick on his table is jotting down on his diary. I am roaming hither and thither frenziedly. I am looking at the wall. No, neither there is a trace of the spider nor her web.

I come out of my hole carefully. Jump at the table, roam about in the bookshelf, hop at the dark corner of the room. No. The web is completely wiped out. At places of course on the wall, tiny traces of the web still feel sticky, diffusing distinctly the fragrance of the spider. I roam madly as if to convey the spider that, a cockroach does have a heart, needs to have one. It echoes through out the room that a cockroach too has a heart, a heart, a heart, it has a heart, a heart, a heart.

Into my hole I retreat silently. Since long the lad is asleep on his diary.

CHAPTER SIXTEEN

Four years in jail

Many exited this jail. I too attempted many times. But, succeeded never. Neither the doors are firm nor are the sentries alert. Besides, there is no restriction to go out of the Jail. Only, one needs to apply one's wit to find the way out.

Many times I have climbed up the walls. But, failing to jump over, I have fallen back inside. Everyone tries for the initial three to four years. A few jump over and escape. Rest all, get tired and resign to the rigorous imprisonment for life.

"Jail is essential for survival."

The more one's quantum of offence is a better prison one is stashed in. For different jails, different courts are held at different time. One's offence in details, address proof and other documents are produced there. Judges of various statures sit for days together to scrutinise the documents of the offenders. They, by posing various irrelevant questions, try to assess the intellect of the offender. On the day of my hearing, the judge was sceptical of the allegations levelled against me by seeing my facial aspects. My appearance barely suited my age. So, to make the process easier, he asked me the price of potato. That day my heart was thudding in fear. I was unable to meet the eyes of the judge. The shorts inside my dress drenched in sweat. Mistaking potato as earth, I replied, "oblong like a citrus." I could not mark if he was content with such a reckless reply. Then he put me two to three complex questions on current affairs of the country, market price and weather conditions. I was ignorant about their answers. So, I reciting a short poem relevant for the situation, tried to explain my answer. He was pleased with my audacity and said,

"Bravo! Considering your early age, your crimes are of no petty order? You, in future may commit deadlier crimes than these and find place in better jails. You have a lot of time in hand. Go. Do try it." I had no idea what I should do next. Stillpondering over whether I should fold my hands at him or not, I retreated.

After a few days, came a letter from the jail authority. With shaky hands I opened it. Wiping the sweat off my face, and exhaling a few sighs, I read the letter.

"Being pleased with your offence, we hereby assign a place for you in our jail. Occupy the cell with in fifteen days of receipt of this letter, failing which we will assume that our prison is not up to your choice. We will be free to assign the place to the next offender. We congratulate you for your success and welcome you on behalf of our jail."

I pondered to have a check of the jail before entry.

The doors of the jail opened at ten o'clock. The jail authority took me personally to show me my cell.

Other prisoners were stupidly gazing from their respective cells. Pitch black windowless walls along with deep darkness hugged me and clung to my body. Being disgusted of that embrace I shook all of them off my body. I asked, "Is oxygen provided to these cells?" Other prisoners guffawed. I asked one of them, "How long since you have been here? How many times did you try to escape? How do you feel now?"

The bemused prisoners laughed at me,

"You have to get in, to learn everything."

They were as if inviting me, "Come on, you too slave with us, rot with us."

It was not a prison but my grave. It was not a cell but my coffin. I requested the jailer to reserve a pair of hand cuff for me and promised to return soon.

Everyone was pushing me into the jail. My mother forced me to go ahead. My father compelled me to move ahead. My siblings also forced me to move on, "Some or other, a jail is essential these days for survival. Of late, there is a ceaseless struggle for a space in a jail."

They were not prepared to pay a heed to me. A few friends considered me lucky, a few teased, still a few envied. But none was prepared to listen to my point of view.

The day of starting for the jail was nearing. I went thorough all the yellow letters. I relished on the acquainted faces pasted in the old album. I mourned on all the care-free days. Recalling the face of my beloved, I pondered over her. Remembering my parents, siblings, friends, my dog, goats, cows, calves, parrot, the tank, mountain, forest, the open sky, the moonlit night and the pretty faces, I shed copious tears. The days of getting into prison was approaching. I wrote down a host of letters and sent them to friendsannouncing my imprisonment and sneaking away from home, took a tour of my beloved's place.

She was elated regarding my imprisonment. She was as if in the seventh heaven. Perhaps she was dancing, singing and gazing as if at the cost of her senses.

"Are you not sorry with my imprisonment?"

"Oh, so quickly you got a place in jail, shouldn't I be happy?" I was absolutely livid with her. Out of anger and grief, I was dumb. She, handed me over a glass of hot coffee, held my hands and searching for something in it said, "I wish, I could pay a visit to the temple. You know, how much I begged before Him that may you be imprisoned as early as possible."

"Aren't you sorry that, we may not meet any more, that we cannot gossip freely, that we cannot roam about freely?"

"Jail is essential for survival," You know.

There was nothing left for me to whisper or holler out at the deaf ears. They were all laughing at my grieving. I spited at their kinship and screamed in mind. The day of imprisonment had approached.

One day, all my kith and kin, friends and siblings dumped me in a train and bade me farewell asking along to write and remember them occasionally. A few even shed a few drops of tears for me.

Like a sack of rice, I lay at a corner of the train. With dreamy eyes, I was looking outside the compartment, at the forests, at the open sky and the moon through the window. I was cherishing my past, bemoaning them, weeping, wiping tears and swallowing the spittle. That day my relatives while loading me off in the train repeated, "Jail is essential for survival."

The jailor verified all my credentials and took my signature on a declaration paper that, I have agreed for the rest of my life to sell my spirit and abide by the overlord. After a thorough examination by a doctor from tip to my toe, my height, weight and width of my chest he said, "No need of a bunch of such nice lush black hair on this head." A barber was asked to, wipe all the evil ideas out of it and pour in some raw ideas of the jail.

I was shaved off. For the initial few days, one staff, hammering on my head tried to adjust me into the environment of the jail. One day, the officer calling me near asked affectionately, "My Dear chap! How do you like the jail? There is no better jail than this one. For a few days, you may feel awkward, then everything will seem normal and natural. You will get used to it and enjoy your stay. Until now, you were flying high unrestricted since you had wings. For a few days you will feel out of place. Your wings will flutter. It may be painful. You will be desirous to break loose. But, gradually your wings will slump. You will forget about your wings. One fine morning you will find that suddenly your wings have vanished. Still you may keep on trying, if at all you wish to escape."

He, after a long deliberation, on a short history of the jail and a brief sketch of some of the inmates, introduced me to some of the jailbirds and explained me out my jobs.

"Basically two types of works are carried out here. Both are, of course, of similar nature. One is counting of sticks. A few bundles of sticks are there. A few come in, a few go out. You have to take in cautiously, counting the sticks, pay them out carefully and re-bundle the balance quantity. Next job is to keep an account of the bundles of sticks. We have got an account of the bundles of sticks. A few bundles of sticks go out, a few come in. You, applying your brain, using your intellect, have to tally the balance by adding, subtracting, multiplying, dividing, mixing and stirring and keep an exact record of the source and quantity of incoming and outgoing sticks. Besides, there are other types of activities too, for which your wisdom has not ripened yet. For the moment, you do this much only."

Since that day, I have been rotting in the jail. I count from one to hundred, keep the accounts, bundle the sticks and repeat again from one to hundred. Many attempts of escape have crowned with failure. Since that day, I have been lying within the pitch black dark walls devoid of windows. I have wailed pitiably, moaned in pain, climbed up the high walls, fallen and bled.

At times, a few come to see me. But, I don't have time to see them or reprieve from counting and bundling of sticks. I look at them through the bars of the jail and sigh. My father calls me "Come!" My mother calls me "Come!" My village hails me "Come!" I run up to the gate. Strike my head against the rails. The jailor gives a tug on the rope tied around my waist. I go back, again start counting the sticks. At times, floats my beloved's face over the piles of sticks. I sit stunned for sometimes. Someone hammers on my head. The nights become a burden on me. I miss the sky, I miss the moonlit night, I recall the tear filled eyes of my beloved, the river and weep uncontrollably. I bang on the walls and scratch on the floor. Neither a wall breaks nor opens up a hole to have a look of the sky.

For a long time my beloved wrote to me about her tears and sometimes along with drops of tears she sent me dried flowers of the temple in letters.

Initially I too wrote her beautiful letters back. But very soon, she objected to them as sheets of interest statement or accounts of profit and loss. Calculation had replaced my narration.

I know no more, what goes on in the world outside. I remember no more, how the moonlit night looks like. The blur faces of my parents, my beloved, my friends and siblings come out of the stakes of sticks. Their voices punch me on my heart; pickle me in the jail, "Jail is essential for survival."

I scream, please someone, stretch your hand, save me from this jail. Smile and laughter gush out of every face - my head I strike, helplessly I weep. I crawl in the darkness, bite the shackles, bang and kick the walls, scratch the floor with my nails, crush my teeth, yet neither a tiny hole ever opens up anywhere nor visible a stretch of meadow or a span of sky or even a shade of moonlit night. I keep on crawling in the darkness and gazing at the darkness like a stupid.

CHAPTER SEVENTEEN

A phase of calumny

Don't know why, but nothing delights me. I can not escape my troubles. When, solution for one trouble I search out, crops up a new one to disgust me. I am unable to act upon my plans. An emotion of failure deters me from taking up a new step. In spite of all my efforts and care I know that, I cannot achieve anything.

Earlier, it was not like this. I, times and again, pondered over my failures of last few years but could not trace out the reason behind them. Previously, everything was plain and easy. My wishes could be fulfilled effortlessly. But, how come everything could go topsy-turvy with in a span of just two years?

Consecutive failures made me superstitious. By the order of my wife, a few *pūjās* were held. My wife herself observed *Sixteen Somavār, Samkrāntī Puja, Śani Meḷā* and *Santoshi Vrata*. I too had to waste a lot of time entwined in her irrational beliefs. Non vegetarian food at home became a taboo on certain days of the week. Still the situation didn't improve. I stayed sunk in my troubles. At last, losing all faith in sectarian rituals I resigned to my fate. I resolved to face life as it came to me.

My wife was not yet desperate. She continued with her endless planning and at intervals tried keeping my moral high, "Nothing is predictable. You just stick to your plan. Keep on trying. Everything will smoothen in due course. The past will return back one day."

I pretended believing in her counsel, though I was in a state of complete loss of confidence in me.

My wife, one day showed me a regional news paper, which she had collected from one of her friends. The news paper carried the advertisement of a *Siddha Bābā* (mystic) along with his picture. The advert mentioned that, the Baba was an expert in astrology. He could narrate the past and foretell the future clearly. He could erase all the troubles by means of talismanic rings. Besides, in bold letters it was mentioned that, the Baba would be staying in a pricy hotel of the town for a short period. A short narration of the name and fame he acquired from his national and international tours was printed along with it. The rumour amongst the ladies folks, that the town is rushing to him, that the Baba is truly a seer, that he narrates everyone's past perfectly and that he solves each one's trouble with guarantee, had reached my wife within no time. The spell of the Baba, possessed her mind so deeply that it was impossible for me to surmount her request. Thus paying a fees of fifty rupees, holding my horoscope, I waited for my turn in the queue, before room number forty-two, Aiswarya hotel.

I sat before the Baba. A sort of divine light emanated from his face. I cannot assure if the Baba had taken some facial make up, but he appeared to have descended just now directly from the heaven and sat before me. His face did not carry much of beard. His face glazed due to his fruit juice diet and resembled a freshly plucked apple.

The Baba, looking into my horoscope, drew a few lines on a piece of spic paper. Then he analysed the lines of my palm and calculated. He asked me to gaze at him and fixed his eyes on my forehead. Until then, I was neither aware of the queer mark on his forehead, nor the blue tint of his eyes.

The Baba asked my to utter a number. Carelessly I uttered nine and in an instant realised my mistake. Number nine was inauspicious for me. I ignored, let happen what so ever and focused on the activities of the Baba. The Baba drew a horizontal line, a few crosses and straight lines over it and stopped abruptly looking at my face, as if I had committed some mortal sin. My heart missed a few beats in anticipation, if the Baba detected some incidents of my past. I, neither wished the Baba to know my past, nor discuss them to me, nor I was eager about my future. Because, life becomes tasteless, in absence of a mysterious future. Then, why at all paying fees of fifty rupees, folding my hands I was sitting before this Baba for hours together? I was least worried for the present, as I am living it and I am aware if it. I realised there, for the first time, that every moment, my future is changing to present and the present to past. The Baba perhaps drew the horizontal line for past, present and future and the vertical lines could indicate moments, hours, days, months or even years. Soon after this realisation, I should not have stayed there. But, I didn't have the courage to get up and offend the Baba for fear of incurring his curse. I had to relay to my wife the Baba's divination and for the sake of the hard-earned fifty rupees paid towards fees, I yielded to a mental truce. But the way the Baba stared at me, I was shocked. I presumed that the Baba has learnt some critical matter of my past.

I now pondered over my past misdeeds, of which I should worry. Steadily a blur picture of the past, took shape in my mind. So far my memory reached, I had stolen a few guavas or a few sticks of sugarcane from some place, which is normal in case of children. Once, in high-school days, being prompted by a friend, I had eve-teased a girl, senior to me. Once, drawing a toon of a tooth of my headmaster, I was whipped. Once, sneaking away from home to the nearby town I enjoyed a film without ticket. Once, eating in a hotel I cheated to have paid and quarrelled. Once, during a carnival I lost twenty five *paise* in batting. Once, in college I quarrelled with a classmate for the front seat. Stealthily, I had been infatuated to two to four girls. I, wrote down a poem citing their names and published in the wall magazine in else's name. Once, I wrote down a love letter one night to a girl and by morning, showed it to friends to prove my courage, though by noon I had dropped it in the hearth of the mess. Once in college, I instigated a friend to contest the election and didn't vote for him myself. Once I had shocked my father with my impolite behaviour. Once, on my rude demand for a pair of shoes my mother was appalled. She broke down in tears and despite my resolve to not have the pair, she offered me money insisting on me to go for it. Once, shoving two wicked cats in a sack, I had released them far away from my village beyond the river. Once, just to prove to my friends the precision of my aim, I brutally killed near about a dozen of snakes inside a well. Mercilessly I had clipped the wings of some dragonflies. Once with a few friends, I had stolen two eggs from a pigeon's nest. Once, while playing cricket, knowingly I bowled bodyline to break the teeth of a friend and injured him.

During my service period, just a few times, I had wrangled with my seniors. Once I had signed the attendance register though I was absent from office on that day. After marriage, for no good reason, I had brabbled with my wife once or twice. No, beyond this I don't remember to have sensibly committed any blunder which should make the Baba so serious.

May be, during my student life, I did love a girl from my side. In my opinion, I should have married her. But, when the girl was married off, I had not finished my studies. The girl of course knew that I loved her and expected everyday either my confession or a written letter, both of which I had failed to manage. A long time afterwards, during my service days, she wrote me a letter alleging that I broke her heart. She further blamed that, I should have confessed to her of my love and levelled me a betrayer. Suppose the Baba detected it, what is there to be scared of? Did I really commit a mistake? May come whatsoever, I don't care. Let the Baba speak out, what he gathered from my past.

The Baba was seated in a meditating posture. My mind and heart were anxious. He probably had learnt by now, what was going on in my mind. Did I abuse the Baba that he would hang me? The Baba looked at me as if startled and relapsed to meditation. I became nervous, not knowing the secret of such an action.

The Baba woke up from his meditation and told me in a sonorous voice, "Do you know, you are passing through a very critical phase of life. A mental trouble has been worrying you since long. That's the reason why you are loosing interest in everything and failing despite repeated efforts. But, no where you seem to be at fault. It's all the fault of your zodiac signs and stars. Here, do you see the presence of four planets in one quarter? It's an omen of some major mishap. This phase sways man from the right path. Man doesn't remain in own control. But, your heart is guileless. You are God-fearing. Thus, through a major cursed time, you are escaping with minimum trouble. It's a phase of calumny for you. This time matches Rama's forest sojourn (*Bana bāsa*). You are faultless, yet treated as offender; having everything, leading life of a friar. However, very shortly, you will overcome this phase. But, you need to be watchful and cautious for these few days."

I felt, the Baba was telling me the right thing. I fell flat at his feet, "Save me Baba. I feel miserable. Please relieve me of this torture. Suggest me some remedial measure."

The easiest of suggestions was, to recite the portion dedicated to planet Moon (*Chandra Mahāgraha*) from the Hymns of the Nine planets (*Navagraha Stotra*) every Monday, offer a garland of 108 Wood apple leaves (*Bela patra*) at the Shiva temple and pray Him for remission, wear a blue shirt and a ring with a blue gem stone on it. The blue gem stone was not available then with the Baba and it will be supplied against an advance booking amount of two hundred rupees, for which I then was not prepared. After returning home, I narrated vividly the whole incident to my wife.

My wife didn't neglect a bit in the arrangement of the remedy. Every Monday, I had to arrange 108 Wood apple leaves. In the evening singing the eulogy of the Moon God, I roamed around wearing a blue shirt and donning a blue kerchief. Still, I had a hunch that there is no escape from the calumny.

May be, I have not confided in you. Three years back, before my marriage, I was a story teller. Soon after marriage, I couldnot write a single line. My wife wished me to write a lot, acquire name and fame as a celebrated writer, receive some state level award etc. Perhaps, I didn't have the time to think over an idea to knit a story. Since morning I used to engage in the worldly affairs so deeply that, I didn't find time to think about myself. My wife used to caution me, "See, your friends have become quiet famous writers. What are you doing?" Whenever a story would be taking shape in my mind, some day to day affair would distract me from it. When I reach the table, the plain paper would remind me of the provisions lacking at home. I lapse back to the domestic affairs, fail to get time for writing and a time came when my wife suspected me, "Never were you a story-teller. May be for a false credit you plagiarised else's writings."

This false allegation of my wife that day pained me a lot. Since that day, I have been retrying a story, searching for a plot, waiting for time, but amidst a strict routine of day to day life, the engagements and the struggle for life, is it easy to frame a good story?

But, until I come up with a good story, I don't think I can escape this calumny.

CHAPTER EIGHTEEN

The migrant Bird

Mr. K.Prabhakar Rao. A retired chief manager of a bank. Even after retirement, he didn't idle at home. He was appointed, due to his valuable experience, as a top financial adviser of a private insurance company at Mumbai. So he not only didn't undergo the melancholy due to retirement but invested his days of retirement in the rightmost manner also. He didn't have paucity of money. The pension and interest on his savings sufficed his day to day maintenance. So, it was not out of greed for money but for right utilisation of time that he had accepted the job.

Sitting in the drawing room and scanning through the news paper, he was waiting for the morning tea. Suddenly hearing the beeping sound of the cell phone he extended his had to it. He saw that a message on a Facebook memory has come. Prabhakar babu read the message. His eyes filled with tears. The memory was enough to make him scatty.

It was related to his last year's poster. Prabhakar babu read his own post from beginning to end once again. The post carried the photo of Niladri, his only son. How handsome looks Nilu in the post! Niladri's pet name was Nilu. This photo was of his last year of B.Tech. Days. He wore a sky blue shirt, a blue tie and carried a handsome face. Prabhakar babu had subtitled the obit, "We all miss you Nilu. The mystery of your death is not yet exposed. Today is your fifth remembrance day. I have done to the best of my ability.

But, it's all futile. I know that, you will not rest at peace until the secrets of your death are revealed. But, who in this cruel world values the tears of a poor aggrieved father? Still, I have not lost my hope. I am pursuing the matter scrupulously. The mystery of your death will unfold one day. The criminals will be nabbed. I just live in the hope."

Prabhakar babu shared the post on Facebook and turned at the picture of Niladri in the drawing room. Born on 30.09.1987, Died on 19.04.2021, Boston, USA, total lifespan a mere twenty-five years! Titbits of incidents of his growing age scrolled before the eyes of Prabhakar babu, tears rolling down his cheeks. Prabhakar babu was scrolling down his timeline of posts on the Facebook wall absent-mindedly, the face of Niladri constantly hanging before him. He was unable to see anything else.

Niladri had acquired his B.Tech. Degree from NIITK in 2010 with distinction. He could have done M.B.A. in any institute in India. But, he had higher ambition. He planned to go abroad for M.B.A. degree. His mother opposed. She was unwilling to allow her only son to go overseas. But, she was helpless before the interest of the son. Prabhakar babu, on the other hand was happy. He wished his son to go out for higher studies - let him earn his share of fame. So, he reprimanded K.Subhalaxmi, the mother of Niladri due to her unwillingness, "What a mother you are? Why cannot you tolerate your son moving abroad for studies? Your affection should not deprive him of his higher studies. Unwillingly that day, Subhalaxmi yielded to the insistence of the father son duo."

She thought, "A span of two years only! By some means I will manage. But, if the son doesn't return from abroad?"

She had come across many such stories where the women there entrap Indian boys in love affairs, marry them and don't allow returning back. After all, she was a mother. But fumes Prabhakar babu at her useless thoughts, "Don't you trust in your own son? But, I have enough trust in him, he won't do anything such."

Niladri was that day elated. He had been chosen for the M.B.A. course in the Boston University and he is the only Indian to avail the chance. Out of the thousands of competitors through out the world, only fifty candidates had qualified for the financial mathematics course, Niladri being one of them. That day, Prabhakar babu celebrated with a treat for the entire family at Swosti Premium Hotel. Just a few days were left for visa and passport. Niladri took up the matter himself. He knew that his father has no time for these things. Besides, Niladri was sincere in his jobs. He never neglected them. He was sincere not only in his studies but other activities also. He helps his mother as well at times in domestic chores. He cuts vegetables in the kitchen and makes home for his mother, prepares tea for his father, goes to market for supplies. Subhalaxmi doesn't feel the burden once Niladri is at home. She only wishes her son to stay near by. She wishes him have a small job and stay in and around Bhubaneswar. But, do all the dreams come true? Whenever she thinks of Niladri going abroad, her heart sinks. She, everyday prepares food to the taste of her son. Poor fellow, where from will he get these home made food there?

Niladri's flight ticket had been confirmed. He had finished his packing. His flight was on 15th of May. He will fly to Boston city, far far away from home. Subhalaxmi wept a lot after returning from the airport that Day. While consoling her, Prabhakar babu too wept a lot. The place is distant, out of reach. It's not Kolkata that he can attend on a call. Whether he can come once in a year is also doubtful. Once Niladri left, Prabhakar babu and Subhalaxmi were left alone in the house. The house as if started biting them. They don't wish to have food. Subhalaxmi weeps ceaselessly before the photograph of Niladri. Prabhakar babu scolds her, "Is he still a child that he will be lost somewhere? My Nilu is very smart. He can adjust anywhere. Just wait, he will prove himself best one day. And you will be proud of her."

Niladri truly was a bright student. His professors loved him much. He stood first in the first semester. He participated in every activity of the college and brought honour for it. Be it song competition or debating or paper presentation or football, he excelled in every sphere. Why not one should love such an all-rounder? But, he was gaining enemies in the campus for his achievements. A host of students were jealous of him. Niladri could not feel how a year passed by. He came home in December 2011, for fifteen days only, after his annual exams. The results were out after he reached there. He intimated home that he had topped the class. That day, Subhalaxmi went to *Lingaraj* temple to offer a *Puja*.

The International Trade Competition was scheduled to be held on 23.02.2012 at Toronto, Canada. For the event only six candidates were selected from their university. Four were from China, one from U.A.E and Niladri. Niladri stood first in the competition and returned with the trophy. That day, Niladri became a celebrity of the entire university. He was felicitated before three thousand students. After this incident he became the eyesore of the intolerant gang. Niladri never expected that such a situation may ever arise amongst students. A number of people shook his hand while he walked down. They wished him. Many of his classmates could not endure with it. Especially the other participants could not digest it. As much worried they were not of their own failure, they were worried for the success of Niladri. His success was unbearable for them. While many students congratulated him, a specific group continued to tease him. But, Niladri remained calm and least attentive to them. He belonged to the land of Gandhi and learnt tolerance best. He was bestowed with many great qualities which were absent in those foreign students.

On 05. 04. 2012, Niladri was returning from shopping. The campus was at a sniffing distance away. Niladri got down the bus and walked down. Just at that time, a few black masked bikers attacked him from behind. Niladri fell beside the street in a pool of blood. Before he could understand a thing they all vanished. Later on, with the help of some other students, Niladri returned to the hostel. He took medicines from the campus dispensary and launched a complain with the superintendent through the hostel warden. The superintendent assured him to look into the matter and intimate the police as well though, he didn't take the necessary step in that regard. Niladri silently put up with all the harassment. On that day, he wrote down an e-mail to his father detailing the incident and cautioned him to not share the matter with his mother.

Prabhakar babu, was anxious after this incident. He was at a loss and clueless regarding his future steps. What could he do from such a distance? He wrote down a protest e-mail to the college authority and attached a copy to the Indian embassy and prayed them to provide security to his son, whose life was at risk. But, no one replied back. Henceforth, Prabhakar babu made it a point to call his son everyday and cautioned him to go around alone. He was unable to share anything with Niladri's mother and was compelled to suffer all alone. Niladri knew that his father will be under stress. So, repeatedly he was mailing to his father not to worry. That, he was safe. That he could manage his own security and not worry about him and take care of his health. He assured him that be will be careful.

On 19.04.2012, when Prabhakar babu was getting ready to go to bank, a call from an unknown American number reached him. Prabhakar babu though wavered for a bit, picked the call up. The caller was an Indian boy, "Uncle, I am a pal of Niladri. Niladri is no more. He has been shot dead last evening in the campus." Prabhakar babu could not follow the rest of his words. The earth as if receded below his feet and the four walls of the room reeled. He slumped on the floor in a heap.

When he regained his senses, he was in Apollo hospital. The only sentence, "Niladri is no more" echoed in his ear. Prabhakar babu was unable to reveal anything to Subhalaxmi. If this is his state, what would happen to her? She might die of a heart failure.

Prabhakar babu asked for his cell phone. He ringed Niladri. He still prayed for the message to be wrong. But, Niladri's phone was switched off. He called back to Nilachal, the friend of Niladri. Nilachal detailed him out everything that, around nine o'clock in the night, some boys called Niladri outside the hostel. He went and didn't turn up. And his death news reached by morning.

Subhalaxmi reckoned from the activities of Prabhakar babu that, some untoward incident has happened. She guessed that Niladri must have been in danger and snatched the phone from Prabhakar babu. Nilachal was still speaking from the other side, "Niladri has been shot dead, Uncle, Niladri is dead." Now, nothing remained hidden for Subhalaxmi. Now, she understood why Prabhakar babu, is lying on the hospital bed since this morning. Should she hold patience or loose it? Who else is there for them? She, curbing her tears, devoted herself to the service of her husband lying on the hospital bed.

The Boston police and the Dean of the university were repeatedly calling them to receive the dead body of Niladri. The Indian embassy and the Foreign secretary to US were also on line. Prabhakar babu was requesting everyone to conduct a proper investigation and find out the culprits. After four days, Niladri's dead body arrived. The after death rites were done at Puri. All the news papers published the incident in headline, "Indian Student Murdered in US." Three thousand students of Boston University brought out a silent candle march. Prabhakar babu preserved all the paper cuttings and shared on his Facebook wall.

Prabhakar babu was disturbed. He, as if made it a purpose of his life to fight against such injustice. Since that day, he made it a point to collect news of incidents against the non resident Indians throughout the world and post them on his Facebook account. He writes protest letters to different agencies. He registers his voice on "change.org" and sends petitions to people for signature.

From 2012 to 2020, within a span of seven years, Boston police has failed to trace out criminals in connection with Niladri's death. The American police system has proved to be incompetent in this case. Prabhakar babu has written repeatedly to the University authorities and to the American Embassy and Indian Embassy as well. Every time he receives the same answer, "Investigation is going on. You will be intimated as soon as the culprits are nabbed." Prabhakar babu thinks, when, the smallest crime is apprehended in India within twenty-four hours, how come criminals can go scot-free in the US for long seven years? And still the country even boasts to have killed a terrorist like Bin Laden? At times he looses faith. He becomes sceptical of the entire system.

By now, a comment had arrived on his post in the Facebook. One of his closest friends had written a condolence message deploring the death of Niladri and wished for the mystery to unfold as soon as possible. Prabhakar babu once again was reading what he had posted on 19.04.2017. It was addressed to the foreign secretary, Govt. of India. An excerpt of the same read,

"K. Niladri Rao, an Indian Student was mercilessly shot dead by some unidentified criminals on 19.04.2012 outside Boston University. Even though with the help of the Indians of New York, the Boston police diligently managed to send the dead body, they were negligent in case of their investigation to nab the culprits. Even after five years, not a single culprit has been apprehended. I had handed over the Boston police and the Indian Embassy whatever documents I could gather related to the matter. But, I am yet to receive a reply from any quarter despite my repeated communication. We are still in dark, regarding the murder of Niladri. I am compelled to say that, India takes a lot of interest whenever a foreigner dies here. But how come everyone maintains a silence when an Indian dies in a foreign land? Does Indian life carry no value? Is the life of a foreigner more valuable that our life? I fail to understand why Indians don't get justice. I know, my son Niladri will not come back. But the culprits will carry on more of such acts in future if they are not punished. It's not only the Indians but citizens of other lands also will be affected. I don't speak on behalf of other countries. But at least students of my country must avail due protection. I expect it of the department of external affairs of India. Thank you."

Prabhakar babu also posted the copy of the answer he received from consul general, the ministry of external affairs. It read,

"Dear Mr. Rao! We are concerned with the death of your son at Boston and the consequent negligence towards the investigation. After your intimation we have taken up the matter with the local authority and pursuing with them to hasten the investigation and nab the culprits as soon as possible. We will intimate you. We will keep you apprised with regard to any further development in this regard."

Prabhakar babu had shared this post on the fifth death anniversary of Niladri on his Facebook wall. And since then, he has been reposting it every year. Except a few condolence messages, he doesn't receive any thing more. He only derives a consolation that, despite being an old man, he still has kept his fight alive, against the killers of his son. If not today, may be by tomorrow, the culprits will be nailed. Then only the soul of Niladri will be at peace. That's the only hope of Prabhakar babu that he is breathing.

When Prabhakar babu failed to obtain any help of justice from any quarter, he started an NGO under the name, "*Pravāsi Chaḍhei*"

(The migrant Bird). He donated all his savings to this organisation. The organisation provides dedicated service to the students going abroad for studies. A number of senior citizens are members of the organisation. They don't apply for any government aid. Being involved personally with many non-resident Odia families, they try to sort out their problems. He detects Niladri in the face of every Indian Student studying abroad. No doubt, Niladri could not realise his dream but he has come out to plant smile on the lips of a thousand other Niladris. Prabhakar babu raises voice against their trouble as if they were his own. These days, where ever an Indian Student is harassed, *Pravasi Chadhei* reaches there with a helping hand.

Through this organisation, Prabhakar babu is trying to fulfil the incomplete dream of Niladri. Today is 19. 04. 2019. the death anniversary of Niladri and the birth anniversary of Pravasi Chadhei.

He has got loads of engagements. He got up without waiting for tea and looked again at the picture of Niladri.

The photo if Niladri was as if praying at him, "Dad! I need justice."